DOUBTS

LONELINESS

REJECTION

by

Catherine de Hueck Doherty

MADONNA HOUSE ⬛ PUBLICATIONS

Combermere, Ontario   Canada   K0J 1L0

Art Credit -

Cover illustration: Heidi Hart

Canadian Cataloguing in Publication Data
Doherty, Catherine de Hueck, 1896-1985
Doubts, Loneliness, Rejection

ISBN 0-921440-33-2

1. Faith -- Meditations. 2. Loneliness -- Meditations. I Title.

BT771.2.D64   1993   242 C93-090056-1

Original Publication - Alba House 1981

New Canadian Edition by

Madonna House Publications
Combermere, Ontario
Canada
KOJ 1L0

Printed in Canada

DOUBTS

Meditation 1

There are very few people living who haven't doubted the existence of God. I must confess I did.

Doubt is a strange thing. It comes unbidden, unexpectedly, suddenly. Or, it can come slowly, entering the intellect and playing havoc with it, in a manner of speaking, so that the intellect for a moment or two, suddenly, truly, does not believe in God. Yet, this strange earth that has been plowed and harrowed for a thousand years is the very earth from which faith springs. A very strange and contradictory thought.

The moment when I or you have really made up our minds that God is a mystery, then, out of the strange earth that has been worked so much, so long, so hard, comes faith.

True! Faith is given to us by God himself, in baptism, but we are supposed to make it grow, and we do. Yet, quite suddenly and unexpectedly, the tree of faith which seems to be so strong, suddenly looks spindly and weak. This is the moment to remember the apostle, St. Thomas. If he did not have doubts, I might not have the courage to doubt either. I might know Christ in an entirely different way. Thomas' doubts brought me a knowledge of God that I never possessed before.

So you begin to doubt doubts, a very wholesome occupation! To doubt doubts really brings one closer to God, for he expected and expects to be doubted. In fact, while he was on earth, his miracles and all his speeches were directed to people who obviously doubted what he said.

Take, for instance, when he said: "I tell you solemnly, if you do not eat the flesh of the Son of Man and drink his blood, you will not have life in you" (Jn 6:53). The Jews left him, as many did. Then he turned around to the apostles and said: "What about you, do you want to go away too?" (Jn 6:67) That was the moment of faith.

In doubting doubts you understand something you didn't understand before, and the mystery of Christ opens its doors to you. I have a suspicion, (I probably am wrong) that it is the doubter who knocks at the door of Christ. The "righteous one" who never

doubts, doesn't knock at God's heart. Only those who doubt cry out
to him.

> I fled Him, down the nights and down the days;
> I fled Him, down the arches of the years;
> I fled Him, down the labyrinthine ways of my own mind;
> and in the mist of tears I hid from Him,
> and under running laughter.
>
> Up vistaed hopes, I sped;
> And shot, precipitated,
> Adown Titanic glooms of chasmed fears,
> From those strong Feet that followed,
> Followed after.
> But with unhurrying chase,
> And unperturbed pace,
> Deliberate speed, majestic instancy,
> They beat—and a Voice beat
> More instant than the Feet—
> 'ALL THINGS BETRAY THEE, WHO BETRAYEST
> ME.'
>
> "I pleaded, outlaw-wise,
> By many a hearted casement, curtained red,
> Trellised with intervining charities
> (For, though I knew His love who followed,
> I must have naught beside);
> But, if one little casement parted wide,
> The gust of His approach would clash it to.
> Fear wist not to evade as Love wist to pursue.
>
> Across the margent of the world I fled,
> And troubled the gold gateways of the stars,
> Smiting for shelter on their clanged bars;
> Fretted to dulcet jars
> And silvern chatter the pale parts o' the moon.
> I said to dawn: Be sudden; to eve: Be soon—
> With thy young skyey blossoms heap me over

From this tremendous Lover!
Float thy vague veil about me, lest He see!

I tempted all His servitors, but to find
My own betrayal in their constancy,
In faith to Him their fickleness to me,
Their traitorous trueness, and their loyal deceit.
To all swift things for swiftness did I sue;
Clung to the whistling mane of every wind.
But whether they swept, smoothly fleet,
The long savannahs of the blue;
Or whether, thunder-driven,
They clanged His chariot thwart a heaven,
Flashy with flying lightnings round the
spurn o' their feet:—
Fear wist not to evade as Love wist to pursue.

Still with unhurrying chase,
And unperturbed pace,
Deliberate speed, majestic instancy,
Came on the following feet
And a Voice above their beat—
'Naught shelters thee, who wilt not shelter Me.'

I sought no more that after which I strayed
In face of man or maid;
But still within the little children's eyes
Seems something, something that replies,
They at least are for me, surely for me!
I turned me to them very wistfully
But just as their young eyes grew sudden fair
With dawning answers there,
There angel plucked them from me by the hair.

Come then, ye other children, Nature's share
With me' (said I) 'your delicate fellowship;
Let me greet you lip to lip,
Let me twine with you caresses,

'Wantoning
With our Lady-Mother's vagrant tresses,
Banqueting
With her in her wind walled palace,
Underneath her azured dais,
Quaffing, as your taintless way is,
From a chalice
Lucent-weeping out of the dayspring.'
So it was done:

I in their delicate fellowship was one
Drew the bolt of Nature's secrecids.
I knew all the swift importings
On the wilful face of skies;
I knew how the clouds arise,
Spumed of the wild-sea-snortings;
All that's born or dies
Rose and drooped with; made them shapers
Of mine own moods, or wailful or divine—
With them joyed and was bereaven.
I was heavy with the even,
When she lit her glimmering tapers
Round the day's dead sanctities.

I laughed in the morning's eyes.
I triumphed and I saddened with all weather,
Heaven and I wept together,
And its sweet tears were salt with mortal mine;
Against the red throb of its sunset-heart
I laid my own to beat.
And share commingling heat;
But not by that, by that, was eased my human Smart.
In vain my tears were wet on Heaven's grey cheek.
For ah! we know not what each other says.
These things and I; in sound I speak-
Their sound is but their stir, they speak by silences.
Nature, poor, stepdame, cannot slake my drouth;

Let her, if she would owe me,
Drop yon blue blossom-veil of sky, and show me
The breasts o' her tenderness:
Never did any milk of hers once bless
My thirsting mouth.

Nigh and nigh draws the chase,
With unperturbed pace,
Deliberate speed, majestic instancy,
And past those noised Feet-
A Voice comes yet more fleet-
'LO! NAUGHT CONTENTS THEE,
WHO CONTENT'ST NOT ME.'

Naked I wait Thy love's uplifted stroke!
My harness piece by piece Thou hast hewn from me,
And smitten me to my knee;
I am defenceless utterly.
I slept, methinks, and woke.

And, slowly gazing, find me stripped in sleep.
In the rash lustihead of my young powers,
I shook the pillaring hours
And pulled my life upon me;
grimmed wih smears,
I stand amid the dust o' the mounded years-
My mangled youth lies dead beneath the heap.
My days have crackled and gone up in smoke,
Have puffed and burst as sun-starts on a stream.

Yea, faileth now even dream
The dreamer, and the lute the lutanist;
Even the linked fantasies, in whose blossomy twist
I swung the earth a trinket at my wrist,
Are yielding; cords of all too weak account
For earth, with heavy griefs so overplussed.
Ah! is Thy love indeed

A weed, albeit an amaranthine weed,
Suffering no flowers except its own to mount?
Ah! must-
Designer infinite!-
Ah! must Thou char the wood ere Thou canst
limn with it?
And now my heart is as a broken fount,
Wherein tear-drippings stagnate, spilt down ever
From the dank thoughts that shiver
Upon the sighful branches of my mind.
Such is; what is to be?
The pulp so bitter, how shall taste the rind?
I dimly guess what Time in mists confounds;
Yet ever and anon a trumpet sounds
From the hid battlements of Eternity;
Those shaken mists a space unsettle, then
Round the half-glimpsed turrets slowly wash again;

But not ere him who summoneth
I first have seen, enround
With glooming robes purpureal, cypress-crowned,
His name I know, and what his trumpet saith.
Whether man's heart or life it be which yields
Thee harvest, must Thy harvest fields
Be dunged with rotten death?

Now of that long pursuit
Comes on at hand the bruit;
That Voice is round me like a bursting sea:
'And is thy earth so marred,
Shattered in shard on shard?
Lo, all things fly thee, for thou fliest Me!
Strange, piteous, futile thing,
Wherefore should any set thee love apart?
Seeing none but I makes much of naught' (He said),
'And human love needs human meriting:
How hast thou merited-
Of all man's clotted clay the dingiest clot?

Alack, thou knowest not
How little worthy of any love thou art!
Whom wilt thou find to love ignoble thee,
Save Me, save only Me?
All which I took from thee I did but take,
Not for thy harms,
But just that thou might'st seek it in My arms.
All which thy child's mistake
Fancies as lost, I have stored for thee at home:
'RISE, CLASP MY HAND, AND COME.'

Halts by me that footfall:
Is my gloom, after all,
Shade of His hand, outstretched caressingly?
'Ah, fondest, blindest, weakest,
I am he whom thou seekest!
Thou dravest love from thee, who dravest Me.'

(*The Hound of Heaven*
Francis Thompson)

Return and knock at his heart. At once the heart opens, the doubts vanish, and, for awhile, all is well.

Meditation 2

Well, I do meditate and I do pray and I do think the night before, but not about what I am going to say today or tomorrow or the day after. I never give it a thought. I never give it a thought when I face an audience. The only way I face an audience, is to look at them to see how they feel and how I feel.

But this is a meditation. I don't even want to use the word "meditation" because I am just sitting still, just looking into space, you might say, at all the immense spaces that are outside the window there.

Yesterday I was very much like someone who was in space

because Father Briere very kindly gave me the Sacrament of the Sick for my knee. I had never experienced the Sacrament of the Sick, knowingly, so I was given something out of this world—out of all the worlds of space and time. I was given the tender and awesome Sacrament of the Sick. I felt as if I was lifted up in the arms of God. I felt as if I had been at Our Lady of Lourdes. I didn't care if my knee got better or didn't get better. I was so full of light and joy that it didn't matter, nothing mattered very much.

I have been a nurse, and my nursing was always directed to Christ. I always said: "This patient is Christ. Let us treat him accordingly." And I tried to the best of my ability to do so. I used to come at night to visit the patients. But the head nurse, (her name was Mrs. Halt, she was a wonderful person), forbade me. She said: "You are always visiting these patients." I really loved my patients very, very much. Anybody who is sick has a great appeal for my heart. I said to myself yesterday, "What an appeal sick people must have to God's heart. He cured so many because he loved so many. He loved the world and so he cured all those who came."

It is our lack of faith amongst other things that makes us sick. If we really had the faith of the centurion, we would be whole. And yesterday I experienced the infinite tenderness of God for his sick and the awesomeness of his coming. Sickness manifests itself in strange ways. One can be very whole physically but very sick spiritually. Do we have recourse to God when this happens to us? What kind of a Sacrament do we use? There is the Sacrament of confession. There is the Sacrament (a most beautiful sacrament), of the Eucharist—reception of the Body and Blood after confession. Two arms are open to embrace us. Two lips are ready to kiss our lips, for the Russians believe confession is the Kiss of Christ. But in order to enter into the mystery of those sacraments one has to be converted, one has to be changed, turned around to face God instead of turning one's back to God.

Here we face our greatest enemy and in a sense perhaps our greatest friend. We face doubt. Doubt of his existence. Doubt of his goodness. Doubt of his power. Doubt of everything connected about and with him. We lay out on a table, like a picture puzzle, the pieces of doubt that we have about God. We examine them separately and we try to fit one into the other. Seldom anything fits, but anyhow, we try. And so, because we are ''in doubt,'' or so we think, we let him fall out of our lives just like some tired or sick or emotionally disturbed mother or sister lets a child fall. I think when you let God fall, the world shakes—but that may be simply my writer's imagination.

Still, here before us are all the doubts I ever had toward God. They are strange picture puzzles. They grow little roots and tie themselves to the place of their origin, and they don't want to go away. You have to pull at them and throw them into the fire, for all our doubts apply to God. They turn to ashes no matter how clever we are, how brilliant we are, how fantastic we are.

When you think of Engels, who was the teacher of Marx, and of Marx who implemented the teaching of Engels, what have you got? Marx attributed to religion a thousand evils, and he was right about many of them. They were not doubts, they were facts. We have to be very careful in sifting out facts and doubts. To give you an example: A parish priest is a louse, as far as you are concerned, barely celebrates Mass decently. His manner of hearing confession doesn't appeal to you. These may be facts about his given traits, but that doesn't mean that you doubt all priests. And even in regard to your pastor, you have the faith that tells you that, in him, God exists in his fullness.

Here on one side is a doubt because papa, mama, priests or authority of any kind is a louse, so you think. But is all authority like that? All of us doubt at one time or another. But we must burn our doubts in the fire of the holocaust because we know that our doubts don't exist. They are phantoms.

It is good for us to go into a chapel, or any place, sit down in the evening quietly, and face our doubts one by one, and realize that the road of doubts is the road of perdition. It can lead only to a hell of our own making. I should be the first to tell you, for to bring forth an apostolate like Madonna House, every step in the beginning is a doubt. Only the burning of doubts and the growth of faith, which go together, can achieve an apostolate. Squabbles inside, squabbles outside, cursing of the priests, dislike of bishops, ridiculed by the negro, ridiculed by labor, ridiculed by your own, you are lying there somewhere on a pavement, all bruised and battered. Yes, doubts—new ones and old ones come forth and touch you like a soft kitten's paws. They are around all the time, but what you have to do is throw them into the fire, the fire of God's love. When you love him you believe in him. When you believe in him and love him, you hope. Faith, love and hope sweep away doubts. Try it some time.

Meditation 3

I am sitting in the kitchen. Am I thinking? Am I dreaming? Am I wide awake or am I asleep? God and I right now are not exactly at odds, we never are. But I want to ask him a thousand questions and yet I wonder if I should. I am deeply bothered in my very soul in so many ways. But truly and honestly, I doubt God. It is strange this "doubting God," because I believe in him and I never really doubt. Yet there are moments when doubts assail me like an army in battle array. I am full of fears that they will overcome me. They can't, they must not, because if there is one thing for which I exist since childhood, it is to love God.

I am in love with God, so how can I doubt him? It is impossible. Yet there it is, a strange thing.

Take for instance right now, January 9 of 1980. I have just listened to what I call "newses," the news of the previous day. As I see it, we are confronting Russia. Unfortunately, U.S.A. does not understand many things about Russia, but then, who can understand another unless they love the other. So, I take hold of my beloved Bible and I see what God says. "O God, give your judgment to the King. To the King's son your justice, that he may judge your people with justice and your poor with right judgment. May the mountain bring forth peace for the people and the hills justice. May he defend the poor of the people and save the children of the needy. In his days justice shall flourish and peace till the moon fails. He shall rule from sea to sea, from the great river to the earth's boundary."

In the face of this, doubts assail me. They come from the right and they come from the left, they are in front of me, behind me. I want to scream, and I want to cry. But all I can do is fall flat on my face in some kind of mire, and moan, because I am in doubt of the God that I love. I say to myself, "Doubt is not lack of love. It is just your humanity. You don't love *enough*. You must love more." But my mind churns like a windmill.

"Oh God, give your judgment to the King. To the King's son your justice, that he might judge your people in justice and your poor in right judgment."

Suppose you were lying in a mire, and the wind turned the windmill over you. Windmills screech. Windmills make all kinds of strange noises. The noises blend with the doubts in your heart. Where is this king who is going to do justice? Presumably this must be Jesus Christ. But Jesus Christ *has* come. He rules with justice but nobody listens. Nobody listens. Do you understand that? The Son of our Father who is in heaven, and whom he has sent to redeem us, is speaking the words of truth. But how can I believe? How can I never doubt that what he says will take place? The poor are not judged with justice; they are stuck in some camps, like the Cambodians. "How about the Cambodians," I said, crying out from the mire to God. "How about the Cambodians, how about them?"

My mouth is filled with the mire. I am shaken by doubt. That doesn't eliminate my love for God, but leaves me weaker than weak, yes, weaker than weak. May the mountains bring forth peace, and the hills justice for the people. May he defend the poor of the people and save the children of the needy. Where are those needy? Where are those poor that he is supposed to save? He is not saving anything as far as I can see, and doubts like a thousand-headed Hydra assail me. I get up from the mire, and I shake it off. I must go and find water, find a lake. Taking all my clothes off I enter the lake, for this is still the season of Theophany. Christ is being baptized, Christ is going to the wedding feast, Christ is revealing himself to the gentiles. But I am totally concentrated on washing from the terrible army of doubts. As I dive down into the water and get soaking wet, I return to the shore and find the white garments of faith.

Meditation 4

Yes, I find on the shore the white garments of faith. I rejoice with great joy and I hasten to cover my nakedness with this white, shining, shimmering garment. And I walk down the road proudly. I have faith. Nobody will bother me any more about doubts. I am wearing the white, shining, shimmering Garment of Faith.

My step is light, I hum a song. The road is straight. I come to a curve in the road. Suddenly I ask myself, "Where am I going?" But I make the turn and I find that my white shining garment has changed colours because somewhere in the sky there is a storm coming. The sky is dark and all the plants on the earth reflect that darkness. I stop, but I know I must go on—and I go on. And strange, how terribly strange, I must have walked quite a few miles, but I am in front of a big hole, or so it seems to me. The hole has steps that go down; they are made of wood, ancient wood, very, very strong, and you can see a thousand steps going downward.

There is no other place to go. Not far away, the storm is breaking. Everything is at sixes and sevens. There is some chaos going on around me but I have to go down the steps. But strangely enough I stop. I stop because doubts again assail me, I don't know where I am going. I don't know why I am going. I am utterly lost for a few moments, or is it for eternity? I say to myself, "I cannot go down alone. All the staff of Madonna House must come with me."

How am I to gather them together, so that together we can walk those ancient steps that lead—I don't know where. And so I hesitate for a second, and then I flee in the face of the storm, in the face of the chaos, in the face of everything that frightens me so. Now the doubts have smeared my white robe. And I really am filled with doubts.

But notwithstanding all doubts, I run. But my running is strange. It is as if each step was gigantic. I was rescuing my children at Madonna House. I don't know how I did it, but here I am in the West Indies bringing them back with fantastic rapidity to the old worn steps. There I am too, bringing everybody from the

U.S.A. to the worn steps and surrounded by them I stop again, saying to myself that I am a fool, that I should leave them where they are. And doubts shake me on those old worn steps. Doubts shake me like an ague, like fever: "Should I or should I not go down those steps? Where do they lead? Where do they come out? What is it all about? I don't know."

That very "not knowing" moves me to walk down the steps and I cry out to God. I walk in sheer faith. There is nothing left. Hope is a tiny speck. Love fills my heart, it's true, but faith in God is shaky, for the wind gets stronger and stronger. Now I have made up my mind, or did God make it up, I don't know.

I walked down the thousand year old steps. Down, down, down, they lead to some sort of a catacomb, but I follow them. I follow them because I believe. Against all natural intelligence, against all that people are telling me all over the place, I move. I move fast down the steps, and the staff follow me, and we come to a sort of a subterranean passage. A strange one. It is rather wide, and all along the walls are inscriptions. As we pause for breath, we begin to read the names of the saints that were buried there. Suddenly I look at myself, at the garment that was stained by doubts and mire. Lo and behold, it's as white as a fleecy cloud.

And now I am not afraid any more, and all doubts have vanished. Here I am in the catacombs. We all are, and we can read the names of those who went ahead of us.

There is no fear any more. There is nothing but joy. Joy because the place is holy, very holy. And suddenly the Christ I doubted so much is before us. We all see him walking ahead. It might be a phantom. It might be imagination. But for a moment we see him turning this corner and that, and we follow him quickly.

We arrive at a big chamber, very comfortable, where evidently the saints rested. There is a sort of ledge where they must have slept. And suddenly one of our staff workers says, "How wonderful. Think of all the saints that are here and all the Masses that have been said here; this place indeed is holy." I collect my doubts. Would you believe it? They barely fill one hand. As I look at them, they vanish. There are no doubts any more. Suddenly some priest begins to sing Mass in a very beautiful voice, and I am lost. I am lost in absolute astonishment. Only two seconds ago I doubted.

Meditation 5

It is time to get up. I don't want to get up. Frankly I want to really die. The little room in Harlem contains so many things—a frigidaire that doesn't work, a gas stove that does, a big sink that is more like a laundry sink than anything else, a lamp in the middle of the ceiling swaying a little if there is a breeze. Alas, there is really very little breeze in my room.

But it is time to get up!

Slowly I do. Oh, I have a bathroom attached to my room. The only trouble is that in the summer the water is very hot and in the winter it is very cold. I never figured out from the janitor why this is so. But I use the water sparingly and wash myself in its coldness. For now it is summer. It refreshes me for a little while. I dress and I contemplate breakfast, which I shouldn't do because I have to go to Mass. Slowly and reluctantly, I lock the door with several locks, as you always do in places where the poor live. I cross the street and there is the church. I walk into it, trying to eschew what appears to me like a thousand children playing on the street. There are not enough streets set aside for children to play. Anyhow, the air is polluted. Not only is the air polluted from exhausts, but from all the smells that come from the East River.

But I guess I am used to it. I make my way through the children who all call me "B." It has nothing to do with being a Baroness; it has a lot to do with being a bee. According to the kids, if I pray to the Holy Spirit, he will give them the things that they want— namely, baseball bats and a ball and such. I doubt my prayer. Mostly it is the goodness of the Knights of Columbus and other organizations who provide bats and balls, not me.

I entered the dim church. There are very few people. It looks deserted, or almost so. I look at the statue of Blessed Martin de Porres on the right and Our Lady on the left side. In the middle the priest says Mass. I am just in time.

There are about five people in that big church. I kneel down and try to shake from me the terrible darkness that holds me tight, but I don't seem to be able to do so.

Snatches of the Gospel, and of the Old Testament, keep coming vividly to my mind.

I do not want to leave the church. It is like a refuge of some sort, almost an escape. The priest is saying Mass. The Body and Blood of Christ is being offered for me as well as for the others. This is the time to believe. This is not the time for doubts, for non-surrender, for all the strange emotions that fill my soul.

I try to concentrate. The voices of the children grow louder than the words of the priest. I try to remember that Christ said to let the children come to him. He seemed not to mind their stridency, their questions, their bothering him. You know how children are. They pull at your garment when they want your attention. They yell in one ear and whisper in another. Yes, that's the way of children. And again I find myself praying over so many doubts which occur outside the church door.

The poverty of those people is enough to make one cry. I remember carrying a mattress to an old lady. It was a heavy mattress but I was strong then. I was doubled up carrying it. Some boys stretched out their legs and I fell over them. I bruised myself. They were the poor whom I had come to serve. Everything in me rebelled. Everything in me cried out, ''Take the next train tonight and go back to Canada of the tall pines and the limpid waters.''

Yes, I was shaken by doubts. Have you ever been shaken by doubts so that you wondered why you were even in a church? Well, that's the way I was.

And then from a very great distance, as if it was almost a desert, the air was clear and your hearing became very acute in the clear air. Yes, you heard, ''Take and eat, this is My Body.'' And then, much closer, I clearly heard, ''This is My Blood, the Blood of the new covenant, which is poured out for many for the forgiveness of sins.''

I walked up to the altar railing, I opened my mouth, and received my Love. Suddenly everything was changed. The church was filled, seemingly, with a lovely light, and I returned to my place, the voices of the children stopped being strident and became gay, like the flow of water in Canada. As I came out of the church I saw them, a big forest of children, just like the forests of Canada, tall and slender. They were all laughing and surrounding me and everybody called me B, and I felt sort of proud and happy because of this appellation. Bee, the little insect that goes collecting sweetness from all the flowers. Then my whole apostolate of Friendship House in Harlem became as sweet as honey from the honeycomb.

Meditation 6

So the priest was saying Mass, and all my doubts vanished. That was long ago and far away—so it seems. Right now, suddenly, the night had come. I really did not know if it was night or day in the catacombs, because it was in the depth of the earth. You had to light an oil lamp. There were lots of oil lamps. We have two little oil lamps in our house.

But now it was night. I knew that, because all the staff blew out their lamps. They were all asleep, except myself. I contemplated the beauty of the Mass—the strange ability it had again and again to stop all doubts. And just as I was thinking about it, slowly and quietly, so you couldn't hear them, the doubts returned.

Did you know that doubts have very quiet feet? I sometimes think they wear flannels on their feet so that no one can hear how they creep into your heart, your mind, your soul.

Bingo, they are gone! Bingo there they are!

I said to myself, ''Now stop it! You just had a great grace. God himself took all your doubts away. Now what's the matter with you?'' I was sitting on some stone seat made long ago. It was cold, but I didn't notice it!

And suddenly, out of nowhere, here I was getting up in Harlem when I didn't want to get up. The water was cold in the winter and hot in the summer, nobody knew why. The voices of children were loud and annoying. I was quite cognizant of the fact that I not only washed myself slowly but dressed myself slowly because doubts were filling me up like so many poison snakes. As I was dressing I was asking myself why I was there. What about all those slums? What about God's promises to help the poor? I was surrounded by the poor; they were so tragically poor, handicapped, that my heart wept for them as my mind rebelled.

How I got myself from the catacombs to a beautiful Mass to Harlem I don't know, neither can anybody tell me. It's just that I did.

That is the writer's imagination. I understand now why my husband, Father Edward Doherty, used to say when he was writing a book that he was "pregnant with the book."

True, I wasn't exactly pregnant with a book, but it weighed on me until I finished it. And one of the things that I used to find very hard was this strange ability to move from the catacombs to Harlem.

Now why did I move? I don't know. It was all part of that strange word "surrender."

You know something? I didn't want to surrender. "Surrender" was a very frightening word, and yet it was the word that I thought most about. It came to me in a thousand ways. You surrender when you are in love. It's not merely a surrender of your body. That's lust. That's a passing thing. That's not a surrender. You surrender to a man or woman because you love him or her, and then you see that surrender takes on an entirely different meaning. It is equated with love. Yes, there were moments in my life when I knew that surrender was love.

How did I know that? That's very simple. I looked at the crucifix. Sometimes I averted my eyes from the crucifix because it was a symbol of surrender. Start thinking straight, instead of thinking crookedly: He became Man. That was some surrender! God, the second person of the Trinity, became Man to save us. Think about it! When all doubts assail you like a thousand flies buzzing in your ears and heart and mind and all around you, think about it.

Then he was obedient to his parents; he was obedient unto death to his Father who is in heaven. Think about that, and lay all your doubts before that obedience, then you will understand what the word "surrender" means.

Don't stop. Go a little further. Now he is being crucified. Can you hear nail against wood? Those are the sounds that the doubters hear at night. Nails against wood. He died for us because he loved us. So it is obvious that surrender means love. Do we love? Now that, my friend, is the question. The answer is, "very little," or we wouldn't have wars nor all the tragedies that we are surrounded with.

Love means open arms ready to embrace you. That's what he did when he was crucified.

So think again and get to the very bottom of the word "surrender." You will find that it has no bottom.

Meditation 7

Life goes on its way. Factually, it's a really nitty-gritty affair. Whatever we happen to be doing, fundamentally life is repetitious. Are we looking after babies or children, like perhaps running a prekindergarten, Day Care Center. It's very monotonous— washing diapers, dressing babies, putting them to bed, feeding them, entertaining them the best you can. Well, day after day, it gets monotonous, doesn't it?

So many women find home monotonous. No, it isn't really monotonous, because one's own child constantly is full of surprises, and provides surprises for father and mother. Still, the daily chores are monotonous, if taken all together. Cooking, scrubbing, washing. No matter how a thousand machines may seem to take the monotony out of it, it is still monotonous. We don't know what to do with ourselves sometimes—most of the time. When the machine goes zip, zip, and the machine that washes the dishes goes bloop, bloop, or whatever sounds you wish to put on it, it seems monotonous.

Things have changed so much, and because they have changed, doubts enter, not on quiet feet, but on noisy feet. They have the key to every human heart. Not only women feel the monotony of the nitty-gritty daily living, but men do likewise. I am sure that the President finds, in time of peace, a certain monotony to his job from which he would like to escape by jogging, and sometime does, or by skiing across the country. Sign papers, meet the Congress, don't meet the Congress, be here at this time, be there another time. It can all be just as monotonous as anything else. Yes, from the Presidency to manual labour, monotony can become the path of doubts. Time must be filled somehow. And so husband, wife and children, all feel the weight of this monotony, of this sameness, of this nitty-gritty, daily, doubt.

That is, of course, if they are not in love with God. Then, though they might have monotonous moments of doubts, they are not so powerful nor so devastating. Stop for a moment and think of the daily life of millions of people, from India to Europe, from Europe to the Sahara Desert. Just stop and think how monotonous it is and how easily doubts can penetrate.

Doubts can come openly, one might say, screechingly. They screech within their hearts. It is not a question of being quiet, of pondering something in the depths of your heart. No. It is the rebellion that one feels against the nitty-gritty of daily life.

When we are young we dream dreams; we are going to change the world. We are going to do this and we are going to do that. Yes, all those things we are going to do: But the years go by. We become bookkeepers, or sales clerks. Our job is monotonous and we are assailed by all kinds of thoughts. Yes, the nitty-gritty, daily life of people is the widest road to doubts.

God has given us a small road, a small path, and has bidden us to follow him no matter what, but we can't. There, around the corner, lies the path that is wide, covered with blacktop, bordered by trim trees and permeated with a pleasant air. Our path is full of doubts. If only we could pass a little divide, let's say a little river that has a bridge, to help us out. If only we did that, we would renew ourselves. We would get rid of all those doubts and we would be free. And so there we stand, in front of a bridge, or maybe just another path, that leads directly on that wide, simple blacktop road, where flowers are scented and the pine trees grow tall.

We hesitate, and yet our lives are so dreary, so we think. There is nothing new in our lives. We forget the smile of a child which we suddenly caught and which made us smile in return. We are totally unaware of children calling us to come and play with them. We are too occupied with our ideas to respond to their call. Youth passes us by, filled with questions it wants answered. We are supposed to be the ones to answer them, but we are so immersed in that little bridge, that big blacktop road, that we let them pass by.

We are practically ready to put our foot on that bridge, but we notice casually that there is an old woman sitting by that bridge. She knows all the answers, but we do not stop to find out what she knows. We are going to cross the bridge and find out for ourselves; so we do.

Yes, the average day of man, woman and child, appears to be very dull. Even a child has doubts. He has doubts because his elders doubt. A child is so sensitive that it responds to that kind of atmosphere fashioned by the adult. Yes, there we are, walking on the straight blacktop road. A strange thing happens. The lovely smell we smelled on the other side has vanished and is vanishing more and more. Now we turn the corner and the smell has gone away completely and we are filled with doubts again. Doubts of our life. We wonder, what are we doing on this earth? Thousands of people will die today, maybe millions, and these people will never know our search. They will go on the wide blacktop road and they will find there emptiness. Yes, emptiness. That's where the beautiful blacktop road leads—to complete emptiness.

It is not a question of doubts. We just know that while we travel on that road, it will become empty. Every step that we make is a step by which we lose something. What it is that we lose we shall not know this side of heaven. But one thing we will know. Each time we take that step we lose the clear image of God until finally he seems not to exist any more. And there we are, surrounded by all our doubts, and they alone, strange as it might seem, reflect the face of God.

There is something yet that can be straightened out if we get off the blacktop road into the little path that God has given us to walk on. If we do, we will know that that little path is holy. Now we will catch the smile of a child in both our hands and hug it to our heart. Now we will answer the call of young ones to come and play, and we will answer the questions of those who are a little older. Now all the nitty-gritty days that seemed so monotonous, so full of temptations and doubts, will vanish, and we shall walk barefoot as pilgrims do, down a strange path from which flowers will sprout. Trees will grow around about it, and we shall understand that this is the path that God has made, and there is nothing nitty-gritty about it. And everything about it is exciting, because we will be in love with God. And to be in love with God is the most exciting thing in the world.

Meditation 8

The desert is comfortable. Outside, the desert breaths in the special way that deserts do, and a beautiful moon rides high above the sky. Somewhere at the edges, there is a light, a very tiny light. It is big, but from afar it looks pencil-like. I stand in the middle of our path here and repeat, parrot-like, "Lord have mercy, Christ have mercy, Lord have mercy." I really don't think of what I am saying. I am in the midst of what could pass for a dream but for me is reality. The moon, the light on the horizon, the patio, the desert, they all cease to exist.

I am surrounded. There is a war on and I, being a nurse, follow the sick. This time I have no horse. They have all been commandeered, and the medical officer told me to hurry. So, I sit where the sick are lying, on the very corner of the wagon. It's a big covered wagon, hard, and the rutty road makes it harder.

I cannot remember if there was a moon that night, but I know that there is a moon in the desert. All the outward impressions have disappeared. I live with the inward ones, the ones deeply hidden in human hearts. My first thought is fear. Not so much the fear of death as the fear of being wounded, and also fear for those behind me that lie moaning softly in the night. Fear comes first, then suddenly it vanishes, and doubts assail me like a thousand dancers, as if somebody had arranged a masquerade. Everybody has a mask. I look at all the masks and the hands that hold each other and I know that I am surrounded by doubts.

Out of the very depths of my soul comes a cry, "Lord how did you allow this charnel house to come forth from the earth, for behold, each one of those masked people is bloody.''

Yes, doubts assail me. Doubts in the mercy of God, in his goodness, and even in his ability to stop the war. I look at these dancing figures that are so horrible, and I know that I doubt, I doubt deeply and profoundly; I cannot understand.

Why should those young people in their youth die, be killed or maimed. Why? I asked God loudly and clearly, ''Why?'' and the echo brings my why back to me. I am shaken, shaken in the corner of a covered wagon in which lie about ten, or maybe less, wounded people. I who sit on the very corner of it, I am shaken, not so much with the horrible road we travel, but I am shaken as with a fever, for all around me the masked ones have disappeared.

But here all around me lie the bones of my doubts. God who promised to look after the poor, the sick, the lonely, is false to his promise. How can it be? God cannot be false to anything because he is God. And suddenly I find my face wet with tears. I am encircled with those doubts. They come closer and closer and closer. It is as if now, any minute, I shall die in the arms of my doubts. Have you ever felt that way? Have you doubted when great catastrophes befell your country? On the people that you love? Have you doubted?

Well I did, and it would be a lie to say that I didn't. I really doubted the very existence of God. And right in the midst of my doubt I am lifted up, high above all clouds, above all doubts, above all tragedies, and I nestle myself between the wings of the Crimson Dove, the Holy Spirit, and a great peace comes upon me. And I understand, that it is we who have brought about the wounding of our soldiers, the widows, the orphans, by entering into another war. We always enter into another war. It is our will that does it, not God's. The torture of my doubts falls away from me. I repeat, I nestle in the Holy Spirit's wings like a child nestles in his mother's arms, and all is peace.

Meditation 9

Did you ever feel as if the earth was moving under your feet? Not you walking over it, but it moving under you? Fast, fast, fast, so fast that you could not catch up to it with your own feet? Did you ever feel that way?

Did you ever feel as if life was not worth living? Did you feel the days following days in that kind of monotony that I described a little while ago, a monotony that becomes unbearable? Did you?

Did you ever stand still and suddenly become besieged with every doubt that ever surrounded man? Did you ever visualize yourself a skeleton reposing in the earth, slowly disappearing into the dust and while you were lying there, hear the words "Dust unto dust?"

Yes, did you ever sit quietly in your room, all by yourself, watching the sunset fade away and count the doubts that you had about God?" . . . "Does he exist? . . . If so, why doesn't he manifest himself? . . . Not necessarily in miracles, but in the truths that were enunciated in the Old Testament and the gospels? . . ." Then there seemed to be at such moments a total emptiness taking hold of you. . . .

Yes, the doubts assailing you are real; they are many, but you can't shoo them away. They swarm around you like flies on a sunny afternoon. Perhaps you haven't got the strength to lift the fly swatter. Maybe that's it. Or maybe you just don't care. All these things do happen to people. There are people who believed and hoped and loved. Yet at particular moments, love, hope and faith disappear.

Nothing remains except a darkness: a fantastic, frightening, stygian darkness. You stand before that curtain of darkness and you ask yourself, "Do I have the courage to enter." All around you, a thousand noises, a thousand voices whisper, "No, no, no, stay in the light." But something, something that you cannot put your finger on, something that is almost phantom-like in the depths of your soul and in the depth of your heart, makes you walk.

Then it isn't the earth that is moving too fast for you. No, you walk into the darkness like a soldier walks to battle. You walk with fear in your heart. It is said of fear that it exists to be overcome, and so you overcome it in this stygian darkness. You walk, and on the first step you already know that faith is yours. You plow on. You plow on like a plow against the earth. But you plow not against the earth, but against your fears.

And slowly, you see your fears overcome, you see them all collapse. You stand before this curtain, this dark stygian black curtain, and you remember that you cannot be afraid. You have to walk into this darkness. For when you walk into it you will find him whom you love. But you are not yet aware of it. You make the first step, the second step, the third step, and behold, fear falls from you like a mantle. See, over there in that corner, fear went there and it then disappeared. You overcame it, and now dawn is showing through.

And suddenly there is no more darkness. There is faith, there is love, there is hope, and there somewhere, far down the road is a person. You cannot see from afar if it is a man, woman or a child, but you run towards the person because now you know you have passed the curtain of a thousand doubts. You have understood that at the end of those thousand doubts, lies nothing but faith, love and hope.

Meditation 10

In my last meditation I said that "fear was made to be overcome." You know something? That makes sense, because we are afraid of so many things and most of the time fear holds us tight. Fear of people, fear of involvement, fear of ourselves, and an endless sea of doubts about our security, about our identity, etc. . . .

Whoever said it, spoke well. Fear is made to be overcome because once fear is overcome, hosts of its attendants disappear.

But how does one overcome fear? First and foremost, by prayer. I have seldom used the word prayer in this new book of mine because I use it so often in others. Fear is overcome by courage, too. Courage is not the absence of fear, it is the overcoming of it. We are faced with the same thing all over again under a new guise.

Let us think for awhile. What are we afraid of? . . . Above all, we are afraid of death, of that strange annihilation that occurs to all of us. The brain that functions so well, that talent that was so great, that scientific knowledge that helped humanity in so many ways, all will suddenly cease to exist.

Here is the crux of our fears. Other fears beset our life, but fear of death is the real fear.

Let us examine this a bit. The fear of death is surrounded by doubts. It is the center of it. We are afraid of dying, even in our youth. This fear lays in our lap, as it were, all our doubts of the existence of God. True that's another fear, but it is also another doubt: "Does God exist?" In the face of this fear, where is God? Then one of the deepest doubts begins to fill our hearts. "Where is God? Does he exist?"

Some of us go further, but the majority stop right there and try to forget what they cannot ever forget. Others go deeper. They ask the same question: "Does God exist?" but they want to separate it from the idea of dying. They want to prove to themselves that they are not afraid of death; but they doubt God's existence, and a whole series of questions arise in their hearts . . . he is absent . . . he is not there when needed . . . he inflicts pain most of the time. . . . To serve him is foolishness because serving him means an identification with him. And generally speaking, who wants to be identified with Christ, for Christ always, I repeat, always brings pain.

Yes, that is the essence, the center, of our fears—death. That's the root fear, and we might as well face it. It is the radical fear and the reason for all fears.

But why should we be afraid of death? Death is one of the most beautiful moments of life. If one has faith, the entry into death is a glorious one. It is not a question of seeing angels or our Lady, etc. It really means being greeted by Christ himself, of being invaded by his life, being one with him, "Memento Mori"—remember that you will die, but remember it as a joyful event. God will greet God in me.

Meditation 11

News of war and rumors of new wars are cast about by the U.S. media like birds of ill omen. We are in the midst of doubt. There is no getting away from it. The radio blares; the TV blares. There is the massing of the troops on borders. The arms race accelerates. How is it possible not to doubt? Are there any around us who do not doubt?

I know I doubt, and yet I know also that I love God beyond all loves. I fell in love with God when I was six years old. Because you are in love with God, doubts assail you too. Doubts come from fear, as we discussed in the last meditation; but they also come from the depths of human hell, the hell that man creates within his own heart.

To contemplate the extinguishing of lights across a nation is not an easy thing for anyone to do, but that is how our imagination works. So many of the car manufacturers have put their lights out... Factories are closing in California, . . . where the climate is so very beautiful, . . . where everybody wanted to go, . . . Doubts and fears assail us because there is a fault in the earth that might, even tomorrow, bring about one of the most terrible earthquakes that we have ever seen or heard of. It will be a bigger earthquake than the one in San Francisco in the early 1900's. At that time, that area was not populated the way it is now. It was different.

Doubts . . . like quiet little mice eating up the cheese of my soul, my mind, of my heart. . . I turn around and I don't know any more where I am. Doubts have almost conquered me. I am afraid to go in a plane. I am afraid to go on a train. I am afraid to go in a bus. There are so many planes that collide, so many accidents with planes and trains and cars.

And the water isn't safe either. There is pollution all over the place.

As I sit here, doubts seem to have become part me. Truly, I look at the world and I think, is it worth living in this world? Doubts shake me . . . doubts about the existence of God, his benevolence, his tenderness, his love, his goodness. All seem to have disappeared suddenly in some kind of a green ocean, and I am moving into it.

Yes, I enter the water without the proper diving suit; I feel the caress of the waves on my face. Am I drowning because I ceased to believe? Is that why I am in this green depth? But then, almost when it seems to be that all is finished, suddenly I am lifted up. I am lifted up and a voice out of the green depths, out of the blue-green of the sea, tells me, "This day I have begotten you. I have thought about you before you entered your mother's womb. You belong to me. I am your God. I am your Father. I am your Lover. I am your Spirit. You have been in my mind for all eternity. I have begotten you. Into your mother's womb I have placed you, have received you from her into my arms. I have loved you and I have prepared a place for you in which you will be with me, my Son, and the Holy Spirit, and where our Lady, my Spouse, will teach you the immense joy of being a Christian." Before these words the green depths vanish. Everything vanishes. Only the tenderness of God remains, and the doubts vanish as if they had never been.

Meditation 12

When I think of World War I, when I think of starvation in Russia, when I think of escapes to foreign lands at the expense of one's life, when I think of being present at the break-up of the German Reich and the entry into the Hitler Horror, when I think of Spain and all that I saw there, the abomination of desolation takes hold of me and I stand still in a no man's land.

Yes, I remember. I remember standing still because there really was nowhere to go: mentally, intellectually or emotionally. That is when the abomination of desolation vomits its doubts into your heart as it did into mine. I cried out, silently, because I couldn't bear to hear my own voice, I cried out silently to God: "Where are you? What has happened to You? Where have You disappeared to?"

And then, surrounded by doubts that were deep and profound, I ceased to cry. The doubts of the existence of God, the doubts of his having abandoned us, left me. Even though all around me there were Russian refugees—close to twelve billion of us—and we were only the first ones, the doubts ceased.

Yes, where was God? Anyone who has gone through that abomination of desolation knows what I mean. There are so many refugees these days that they must know, without my writing about it, what it is all about.

. . . But that was long ago. . . .

Slowly, faith reasserted itself, and out of that abomination, out of that desolation, came a knowledge that to follow Christ meant to walk constantly in pain and in joy. Yes, that was long ago, but lately, during these years, slowly, creeping like rodents inside one's head, seemingly busy about eating our brains up, doubts come.

For we are confronted today with nuclear weapons and with nuclear destruction. And doubts, I repeat, like rodents, seem to eat us up!

Oh, with sharp teeth, but not eating up all of us at once as perhaps a lion would, but a little here, a little there . . . and each bite a doubt . . . a doubt in the very existence of God.

It is not a question of accidentals. No, this time the very depths of our faith is being corroded, is being eaten up. There are so many doubts but so few answers! The answers are few because faith must give the answer. But faith surpasses reason, logic, and all the other things that man prides himself on.

And so, in the midst of an abomination desolation, we stand in a sort of a strange middle. On the one side, faith, on the other side, doubts. Doubts seem to overwhelm faith.

This is a strange moment. It's really a crucial moment, for those who believe. Once more, Christians are tested individually. To give in to doubts, to forget all that we call faith, to live a life that is exclusively one's own and has no relation to God, this is not the way. I repeat, the abomination of desolation is slowly creeping upon us, and with it, doubts.

At this moment, when everything seems to crumble within self, an almost suicidal desire comes upon you.

Suddenly, out of the fog, comes a woman, wrapped in silence.

She holds out her hands to you. You put your hands into her hands, she opens the big, beautiful mantle of silence that she is wrapped in. And she wraps you in it herself. At that very moment, even though the abomination of desolation might be all around you, as the mantle touches you, all doubts disappear. The desolation might not disappear because men bring it about themselves, but one thing disappears: doubt!

Yes, when you are wrapped in the mantle of the woman who herself is wrapped in silence, all doubts, too, are silenced.

Meditation 13

Sometimes, the moments of doubt against God, against the Trinity, the angels, the saints, become unbearable. It is as if you had descended into some kind of a pit from which you look upward and you see only darkness. There is no light any more. There is nothing to hold you up. . . . You sit on a knoll and you look into the darkness, and in your heart you ask yourself the question men have asked themselves for an eternity: Where is God? Especially now that we have spacecraft that can circle the planets and send back to us all kinds of photographs to show us that apparently there is no human life anywhere in this solar system.

So you consider what you know from the scientific point of view and you say to yourself, "Where is God? . . . On what planet?"

Then a modicum of sense comes back to you, and you say, "Well, God is not on any planet." You knew that anyhow. He is in you, within that strange place called "spirit." And you recall all that scientists have discovered about the human brain.

I personally remember a doctor whose specialty was brain surgery; he was a believer, a Catholic. He had an electrical instrument with which he made a chart of the brain. This chart showed one place which was active whenever the electrical instrument touched it, and the person began speaking of God. It was a spiritual place. The doctor never said anything, he just marked that this was the spot. Think about that as you look upwards where there is nothing but black darkness.

You just read some place that they discovered a skeleton that was thirty or twenty million years old. You say to yourself, "*This* is going to come alive and resurrect as the Gospel says?" Then, for some unaccountable reason, you begin to weep.

It's as if all your dreams were shattered; as if death was really the end. And there you are, sitting on your knoll, doubting again. You have a flashlight. In your darkness, you use the flashlight and you read the Psalms or the breviary, and you read that God is going to do this and that for the Jews, and he's going to shelter the poor and so forth. Then you look at your past history when you tried to bring pity and tenderness and food to the slums. And you wonder again.

Then suddenly, it is as if everything dissolves and there is nothing. Now doubts have really mastered you. You are not sitting on that knoll, you are lying on it, and somebody is beating you to a pulp. Haven't you ever felt that way? You have.

Then, out of the darkness a tree comes forth, a very small tree. And while you're being beaten black and blue by your doubts, the tree grows faster than your beatings. Suddenly, nobody touches you. You are just lying under the immense branches of a beautiful tree.

You know, almost without knowing, that it isn't growing on the knoll or in some soil around you. It's growing from your heart. You lift your eyes and you are confronted with God himself. He says, "You have passed another Rubicon. You have allowed doubts to besiege you. It's through doubt that you find me. Those who do not doubt, do not find me."

Meditation 14

Yes, that is what the Lord said, "Those who do not doubt, do not find me."

It's a very strange sentence, is it not? But at the same time, it's very true; for those who do not doubt are not on a pilgrimage. You can, indeed, believe in God, superficially; but those who seek him, who really want to find the Absolute, as he is, go on a pilgrimage.

It should be a very simple pilgrimage because the way to find God is in the other person. The way to trust him and not doubt him is to trust another person. There is some strange kind of mystery in all this. Why, trust in one person would open immense horizons of love, trust is truly a mystery.

You should kneel before a mystery, and sometime, even prostrate yourself before mysteries. Only God can reveal them to you or to me, and then, in a quite mysterious way. As far as we're concerned, he decrees that whatever we do to the least of his brethren, we do to him. Now that's something to be thought over!

When we enter the desert of doubts, let us stop and pause and understand that we are on a pilgrimage. This moves our souls, our hearts, ever closer, closer, closer, to God. And that strange mystery of believing when there is nothing to believe in, is the key to a complete trust in God and the dissolution of doubt.

But of course we do not have time these days to pray, kneel, prostrate ourselves, or at least, we think we haven't. And so, doubts assail us from all quarters.

For instance, take war, about which there are so many rumors. We are afraid, and doubts about the power of God are rampant. Frankly, we have then to stop and consider. Our pilgrimage must not go any further because if there is going to be a war, cold or hot, let me assure you, we made it so.

Greed, selfishness, desire for power—these are the motivations which cause both hot and cold wars; and who is guilty of them? Men and women are. They still do not cooperate. They still want to possess the goods of the earth that God has placed in it: gold, silver, uranium, oil . . . Men and women do not wish to cooperate. They do not wish to love one another. Once again, Christ is in a boat, crying out, ''A new commandment I give you, love one another as I have loved you.'' Christ is offering peace, joy, love, hope, all things we hunger for; and we disregard them in order to make our factories work and our cars run.

If instead of doubting God, we doubted ourselves, we could

begin a new style of life with small farms, with love for one another, with no desire for power, no lust for acquiring gold and silver. If this would happen, then we would trust God. But it isn't happening, and my soul in agony cries out to God, "Out of the depths I cry to you, O Lord; hear the voice of my supplication."

Oh, if only we would permit his infinite grace to inundate our hearts totally, completely, we would sleep in peace once again and awake refreshed, believers! There would be no more doubts. Go into a sleep to the tune of our Lady's lullaby, and after we woke up, lo and behold, there would be no doubts.

Meditation 15

It's amazing, what the devil can do. All human beings must have, I'm sure, doubts about the existence of God. But slowly, men of the West have begun to recognize that there is a devil. And I think that they're beginning to know that he, to a great extent, is the sower of their doubts.

I confess that there are lots of doubts that are not begotten by the devil. But fundamentally they all stem from him in a manner of speaking. He is the father of doubts, for he wanted to be like God. But he was thwarted in his desire. This might seem very old-fashioned to some. I can picture some ridiculing the ideas I have, but that's all right! There is no problem. Each has his or her own ideas about doubts; and these are mine.

But I was speaking of the devil. Yes. In his heart he begets doubts, and each one of them he sends forth to humanity, so that human beings will doubt, and especially in a way that will separate them from God.

It is true that God said, "Unless you doubt, you will not find me." This is true. We start on a pilgrimage filled with high ideals, and after long, weary miles we begin to wonder why we undertook this pilgrimage. Doubts assail us on every side, and temptations, too, for the devil is not content to sow doubts in our mind. He wants us to follow the path of evil, the path to denial of God. He has succeeded well, lately, hasn't he?

We see the agony of priests who leave the priesthood, of nuns who leave their community, of married people who divorce, of neglected youth who are the children of divorce. You look at it all and you understand that we can go only one step further than this. That one step is the denial of God.

Anybody who meets a person who has denied God becomes a contaminated person. He or she has to have great recourse to prayer and fasting in order to overcome the same temptation. But we forget these powerful remedies; we too, laugh a strident laugh between two cocktails or amidst the sins of the flesh.

We laugh and we say, ''There isn't any God.'' That is when we really seduce mankind, those of us who call ourselves Christians and profess to believe in God. Yes, that's the way we Catholics especially crucify the Lord Jesus Christ with hammer and nails.

That's not doubt. That's giving in to the temptation of the devil himself. This has to be exorcised by fasting, prayer, and total obedience to a spiritual director.

Jesus Christ was obedient to his Father unto death. Now it is time for us to be obedient to death.

Yes, doubts come quickly, but the temptations of the devil are slow in coming, because they need time to mature in the heart. The most tragic picture is the so-called believing Catholic who goes to Church on Sunday, to confession perhaps once a month, who behaves as if he or she were a Catholic, but inside he or she isn't. Such a person is worried about everything, especially profit, preoccupied by greed and desire, worried about what's going to happen to him or her tomorrow or the day after. He or she refuses to let God direct his or her actions. This doesn't mean that one has to abdicate intelligence. No, but one's life must be directed by the wisdom of God. Yet most lives aren't, and that is the great temptation that sweeps the world these days.

We call ourselves Catholics, but we don't care about our style of living, sexually or otherwise. We take bribes because ''everybody does it,'' so why not me? We climb on the shoulders of our brethren in order to reach one more little rung of power, and then we go to Church!

The devil is ever present in that sort of thing. These are not

doubts, which are more or less natural to man; they are temptations, the goal of which is the denial and the rejection of God.

That is why today we see people walking, not as pilgrims but as
zombies, looking for God who is right by their side. This is what we
must show the world: the face of Christ through all the temptations
and all the doubts. We must show the face of God. For this we
exist. It is a hard road; but we have to tread it.

If we continue our pilgrimage toward God, in God, with God,
then the road, though it be a narrow path, smooths out, and we
enter into the heart of Christ.

Meditation 16

Doubts again! A wind! The kind of which doesn't exist on earth
. . .a hellish wind.

A priest stands alone in the midst of his doubts. They lie around
him as if they were paper scraps from a garbage can, until he is
almost ankle deep in all the doubts which whirl about him.

Somehow he has begun to overcome his doubts. He prays. He
fasts. He struggles mightily against all these little papers upon
which are written down the opinions of so many scholars and
theologians. Now he struggles not only with his own personal
doubts but with a barrage of winds and ideas which leave him
reeling and exhausted.

He's exhausted. If he stands, it's only because he is too tired to
fall down. He cannot move one foot in front of another. He is too
tired.

The hellish rain of bits of paper continues to fall around him.
Now they are knee-high, and slowly they rise up to his breast.
Tomorrow or the day after, they'll bury him, in the bits of garbage
paper. The world seems brown to him because he passes through
the desert. It kills all vegetation. The sun beats mercilessly upon his
heart.

Now another wind comes, but it is a gentle breeze that caresses
his tired face and somehow gives him to drink and even to eat.
Slowly the face of the priest rises and his mind begins to clear.

Someone hands him a broom, or is it a limb of a tree? He starts cleaning a spot around himself.

He stands between two winds. The angry wind which tries to destroy him, and the gentle wind which pushes the other one away. The priest awakes, or seems to. He bends down and gets a handful of scraps of paper and begins to read the words that are written there. Slowly, but very slowly, a strange peace returns to him. He realizes that he was standing in the hallways of hell.

These scraps of paper were written by him who always disguises the power of his hand. Each paper speaks of doubts of the existence of God. Doubts of his Resurrection. Doubts concerning his human life, suggesting that he died like everybody else and that his body rotted in the ground. Doubts about his crucifixion. Doubts about all the things the so-called new theologians would write to a priest.

True, there were pieces of paper scattered around at his feet, but each one of them spelled death to his spirit. The priest knows now that this is an attack on the Church. He knows now that this very transparency is a gift of God so that he can see how easily some theologians twist things around. What was, is no more. The freedom that they offer to other priests is a false freedom, a freedom of death instead of life. And now the priest has shaken himself like a dog shakes when he gets wet. Now the step of the priest is firm. He moves with the purpose of faith, of love, of hope toward a poor kind of a table. Now the doubts have vanished under the gentle wind.

Still the priest moves toward the poor table. There are two candles, and a saucer that somebody left which can barely pass for a chalice. In a firm and clear voice, the priest says, "This is my Body. This is my Blood." He then holds onto the table, and a hand pierced with nails gives him some bread and the wine from the chalice; he sees the face and the arms of Christ. All is peaceful now. Even the whisper of the scraps of paper had ceased. The sky is clear. The sun is shining and the priest has put his head on the breast of God. There he finds all he has been looking for.

Meditation 17

How beautiful is a bride; how lovely a groom. The white of the bride connotes virginity. Two people are getting married. They are supposed to love each other exceedingly. That's why they are getting married, so that two loves might blend into one, two bodies become one.

Of course there are doubts. There are always doubts about a vocation, or shall we call it a commitment. There is always a little doubt when one engages in a commitment for life. So groom and bride probably had their moments of doubts before they were getting married, but love, if it was love, overcame it.

But time went on, and strangely enough, as in so many cases, doubts grew, which meant that trust was diminished. Suddenly those who were supposed to be one before God, (which of course they were, but didn't want to face) decided to separate.

The doubts multiplied. She didn't trust him; he didn't trust her. He didn't like the way she nagged; she didn't like the way he was absent all the time. Whatever the reasons, trust was dying.

Did you ever hear trust die? It dies in a strange way in the hearts of men. It curls up like a newborn child, and suddenly, it becomes smaller and smaller and smaller, and then, it disappears. Where? Who can tell? Where does trust go? He and she trusted one another when they stood before the priest, she all dressed in white, and he desirous to build a home with and through her. They trusted one another, so it seemed, and then, the trust vanished, and the doubts came.

They were not doubts like the priest's. No paper filled their house. Nothing. The house was still as it was before. But, slowly, on a strange wind, through the cracks of the house, doubts entered in. Not necessarily doubts about the fidelity of one another, although they were there too, but doubts about the commitment. Men lay in their beds in the depth of the night and ask themselves, "What did I do? I committed myself 'until death do us part'! But that's impossible. It can't be done. I cannot live with this woman." Or a woman thought about the man in the depth of her nights, that she could not live with him. And neither of them stopped to pray and to ask God, ''How does one really commit oneself totally in a total commitment?'' The doubts became real.

They doubted in the dark of the night; each doubted the other and felt sure of their doubts. When men and women are sure of their doubts, hell laughs, because doubts now begin to take definite form. They are expressed in biting, cold, tragic, words and cynicism is born. Eventually, doubts become feet which lead men and women to lawyers.

At this moment, charity weeps over the children who have been born in love and yet, rejected by doubts. Everything becomes chaotic. Far away, the voice of God resounds: ''What God has joined, let no one put asunder.'' But all this is forgotten, and divorce becomes a tool of him who has planted the seeds of doubt in the hearts of the man and the woman.

He laughs. It is so good to see them fall into his net. Yes, he fills the net with divorced couples and presents it to Jesus Christ as a net filled with a thousand fish, mocking what Christ told his apostles.

Human law allows the two who once loved, who once begot children of love, to be free.

The second Person of the most Holy Trinity walked this earth; so did his Mother. Jesus Christ comes riding on a donkey and comes across a man who has been beaten by robbers. He picks him up and brings him to the inn. There is a moment in the life of man when he knows that he is wounded, God holds him in his arms. Maybe because of this, because of the inn, those who were once one flesh, one blood, will come back again together.

So when God bends down to the man beaten up by robbers, hope springs in the heart of those who love God. And prayer ascends like a dove into the hands of the Father.

Meditation 18

Doubts have begun to march like armies, armies that are so dense that you can barely distinguish one soldier from another, especially in the twilight zone in which doubts walk these days.

Political doubts. Spiritual doubts. Intellectual doubts. An army marches shoulder to shoulder; men and women in the world are lost in that army of doubts. Never before has hell sent such an army!

This army moves, quietly, and it enters the mind stealthily. Before one realizes it, one is invaded by this army of doubts. "What shall we do?" questions the mind. "Are we about to have a war with the Soviet Union?" "Should we be friends with the People's Republic of China?" A thousand political and intellectual doubts besiege human beings whose restless sleep can make hell laugh.

Before the carnage of the mind and the heart, a chasm opens. For the army desires to attack on one point, and one point only: "A new commandment I give you: that you love one another as I have loved you." The voice comes from everywhere, and for a moment, the doubts are stilled, but only for a moment, because we realize that we do not love one another. Nation is pitted against nation, and the only thing that rules the world today is greed. Communism is just another form of greed.

Yes, it is a strange army that slowly penetrates the mind's ramparts and finally reaches its goal. Yes, doubts about the political wisdom of nations is deeply embedded in the hearts of people. It's no use saying that the Soviet Union has no doubts about their government. They do. They hate it. Some nations are ready to translate doubts into fratricidal wars.

Doubts seem to rule everyone. But every person who believes in Christ knows deep down in his or her heart that doubts persist because he or she has set aside God in his or her life. God does not rule the nations any more, or so people like to think. That's why the scientists themselves don't know what is what. They come to the conclusion that there *might* be a God who has created this universe; but the scientific world is filled with "maybe," and "perhaps": words of doubt.

Children look at their parents and hope that their parents are sure of something, someone, that they have no doubts about the fundamentals of life, especially God. But parents are indifferent. They are occupied with themselves. Moreover, millions of children are children of divorced parents.

Where is escape? Where a place, a spot, where doubts will fall asleep forever? There is only one place where man can find peace and the absence of doubts: in the heart of the Trinity.

Meditation 19

So we really live amid doubts. They whirl around us like autumn leaves falling from the trees, making whispering sounds with each step we make. They encompass us sometimes like a quiet rain, sometimes like a hurricane. They leave us rudderless, without oars in the middle of an unknown river. The trees along the shore seem to bend toward us as if they wanted to send doubts across the river.

Yes, doubts encompass us all the time. Strange isn't it, that we doubt so much. It comes down to this: doubts are a lack of trust. I might trust my husband or my wife. Then my imagination works overtime on his or her smallest faults. Doubt overcomes trust. When doubt overcomes trust, then love and hope shrivel up just like those autumn leaves that whisper under our feet. They become brown, dusty, dead.

Doubts are stepping stones to total trust in God and love of him.

But suppose we do not walk beyond those stepping stones? Suppose we pause somewhere in the middle and allow doubts to have their way. The Old Testament, the New Testament, annoy us. We doubt everything pertaining to God. We fall into a general doubt, the authority, that may interfere with our life. And while still sitting on those steps, in the twilight of a gray day, we doubt ourselves and the purpose of existence. These kinds of doubts can lead many people to jump off the Golden bridges of thousands of cities.

Then again, it might not lead to suicide, but it does lead to depression, to all kinds of emotional problems orchestrated by the devil. Emotional illnesses can completly spoil a human life, and they do so because emotions have overcome faith. Once the emotions overcome faith, then a lot of things happen. Then the rustle of autumn leaves under one's feet becomes like thunder in one's ears. There is but one thing to do when this happens, and it is to plunge blindly into the waters of faith as Jesus did. There is no other answer to those kinds of doubts.

Meditation 20

Yes, we have discussed a malady of our age. Perhaps the virus of doubt began long ago, but it has come to full maturity now. And so, man is confronted with himself; alone he faces his doubts. Sometimes he cannot take it, as the saying goes, and he shares it with someone else—a priest, a fellow worker, a wife, a girl friend. But now, coming to the end of these meditations on doubts, (which incidentally came to me in the dark hours of the night) it seemed as if the Lord is saying, "Write about their doubts, because everybody doubts everything and everyone today, especially my Father, me, and the Holy Spirit." Yes, this is the hour, then, of shedding our doubts. This is the hour of prayer. Doubts are silenced only by prayer. You will be surprised how small they are. They're like little chestnuts, falling in autumn, crushed underfoot by faith. They really do not matter at all.

Miraculously, man knows that he cannot doubt any more. He believes with his whole heart in the Triune God and in our Lady and in all of the Church's teaching. *He believes that in them is hidden the answer to all doubts.* By belief we become men of faith, men of Christ.

He said, "Whoever acknowledges me before men, I will acknowledge before my Father." Now is the hour. Doubts fall away, and Christ is acknowledged by men, women, and children. Now faith has spread its wings and chased away all doubts. This is the moment of joy. It doesn't matter that it might be also the moment of pain. Joy overcomes pain, because now we suddenly know that all the while we were in darkness, knocking at all kinds of doors, Christ was there. So we stopped knocking and fell prostrate before his face. Somehow we knew that he would come to us, and he did. Those who shed their doubts through faith know the resurrection. It is only when you really doubt, and things are in the twilight zone, that we realize what the resurrection is.

He rose on the third day. Because he did, I have no doubts. Nor should you have any, for the simple reason that, obedient to his Father, he came to us, the sign of reconciliation under the sign of the Cross. He died for us, and was buried for us, and then, on the third day, he arose. When faith conquers, doubts disappear. Alleluia! Alleluia! Alleluia!

LONELINESS

Meditation 1

There are many kinds of loneliness in the world. We do not distinguish all of them because we do not have the courage to do so. We lump them all under one word, and call it loneliness. And yet, we should differentiate.

There is the normal human loneliness that simply looks for the companionship of another human being: someone to have fun with, someone to share one's thoughts with, someone to share one's pain with. This is the normal type of loneliness. This loneliness can be eliminated, swallowed up by normal friendships.

This is the friendship between the young and the old which one often sees in various parks. Young people are prone to cluster around an elderly lady or gentlemen who is telling them wonderful stories. There is also a friendship among peers with whom we can share the thousand things that pass through our heart, mind, and soul, year after year.

Yes, this type of loneliness can be swallowed up by friendship.

Yet unfortunately, today, friendship is very hard to come by. People do not make friends any more. There is television, the mechanical friend, which, above all, promotes things to buy, and is probably responsible for inflation and recession. And even if it is not, in the long run it is a monster that swallows up people wholesale. TV precludes any type of friendship except the empty greeting, "Hi how are you? Have you seen the latest program?" One returns loaded down with packages from different stores, sets them on the table, sits down and nonetheless remains in an abysmal loneliness.

Then, there is the kind of loneliness begotten by machines. Man needs more than machines. It will not be long before men's minds themselves will be computerized and then, in a mannner of speaking, they will cease to function normally. Yet, loneliness is stalking the land.

One of the most terrible sights that anyone can behold is that of old people living on a meager pension. It is barely enough to feed them. Slowly, they decline into an abysmal state of loneliness. During their last years, none of their children came to visit them;

one can see how loneliness eats them up, as cancer does. Yes, there is this kind of loneliness which is very prevalent all over the world, especially in the western world.

There is a vast difference between loneliness and solitude, an incredible difference between loneliness and those who choose to enter into the silence of God. These two must never be confused, because their confusion leads to more loneliness, to defiance of faith.

Let us look a little closer at the sickness of this world which is loneliness. One can go to one's doctor and discuss a thousand symptoms, emotional or physical. But only a few doctors as yet seem to understand that many of the symptoms you present to their wise eyes are really the symptoms of human, natural, normal loneliness . . . the seeking of a friend, the seeking of someone who understands, the seeking of someone to cry with, of someone to laugh with.

How many of my readers, right now, reading this passage, feel the desire to write to me? I know that they do, because, you see, having fallen in love with God at the age of six, I have fallen in love with mankind—men, women, children. All of humanity is dear to my heart. I understand loneliness. There might be people who are lonelier than I ever was or ever will be, but I have learned to differentiate between solitude and loneliness.

But, friend, I love you. You know I do and, even if you never write me, remember that there is someone in the world who really loves you, and, strangely enough, understands you.

We are talking about loneliness. Take, for instance, the loneliness of the clergy: cardinals, archbishops, bishops, and priests. They, too, undergo a certain type of loneliness. They seek friendship just as anyone else does. Everyone must bear his or her cross of loneliness. We are all mixed up in this world, but in our age there is a particular kind of loneliness unknown to past generations. We don't know how to make friends. Sometimes we are almost unable to make friends. Between us and friendship lies miles and miles of electrical cords and electronic circuits.

There was a time (older people can tell you), when people were neighbors. They did not sit glaring at television with a glassy stare.

No, people were neighbors; and they used to visit each other, or play games together, or other kinds of entertainment.

There was a time when people painted, wrote books, and opened their souls in thousands of ways to others. People could talk and think together. One could read a book, see a picture, view a display or an exhibition. Today we can still see an exhibition or read a book—that is still possible—although very soon books may be read through electronic recordings and there will be nothing left.

Loneliness is almost a part of us. We cry for release to a heaven that at times we even refuse to believe in. Someday we will understand that we have become prisoners of computers. Someday, we will arise and destroy their fascinating power, and we will be free again; we will be able to communicate with others. Our natural loneliness will disappear someday. Yes, there are all kinds of loneliness.

Meditation 2

Yes, we are prisoners today. Prisoners of so many things. And then again, are they ''things'' or are they states of mind? But whether things or states of mind, doesn't make any difference. We are prisoners of technology.

On the horizon appears quite clearly the domination of the machine over man. It gives a nightmarish quality to life. Large newspapers, and even small ones, offer computer dating. To find one's mate, one does not need love or anything else: one only needs a machine. In large letters the ads read: ''Meet your date through a computer.''

Loneliness can throw two people together in illicit lustful embrace. Lust spells tragedy, no matter how you approach it. Truly, we have become prisoners of technology. But this is only the beginning. Unless we smash it and become free again, freedom will cease to exist. Loneliness tears human hearts apart until they cease to be hearts.

Have you ever thought of or prayed for a terrorist, or for a group of them? They use all kinds of machines, and are technologically equipped with bombs and explosives to kill others. True, they have goals, or so they think. "Liberate this or that country. Kill this man . . . maim this one." These are the people whose nights are spent in loneliness. They have no days, only nights, because their days are as dark as night, stygian, hellish nightmares.

And so, I pray for them, because nothing can be equal to the goals terrorists set before themselves: to kill, to maim, to disrupt, to disregard men and women and children. That must be the loneliness of hell, the hell that man makes for himself. And because their cause appears to them to be viable, possible, perhaps attainable, their loneliness is doubled, for deep in their soul they know that this is not the way to peace and to love. To die for a cause appears beautiful, but the cause itself is not beautiful. To die for love, to die for God, to die for peace—that is beautiful, and for this we must pray. There is no lonelier person than a terrorist.

Loneliness stalks every street, every dinky little alley, and every palatial home. These may be barricaded with security guards, for those with money think that they are safe.

Juntas of every kind, trying desperately to hold on to power and wealth, still keep people imprisoned in their poverty. I do not envy the loneliness of the rich man. Nor do I envy the loneliness of a miser. I also think of the Hunt brothers who at one point in their lives collared and collected the silver of the world, only to create a panic in that world. Perhaps they can sleep well, but I would not want to enter their loneliness.

Loneliness abides in low places and high places. However, we are talking about you and me, and the ordinary people of the world; or are we? For there are not any "ordinary" people; everyone is "extraordinary," because everyone has been created by God, and therefore is someone to reverence. Unfortunately, we have despised God's creation in ourselves. We have despised his love, his cross, his life, the life of the Second Person of the Most Holy Trinity. All this we have thrown away, as men throw away a bag of garbage. But now, we slowly begin to wonder where we put that bag. Slowly, we have begun to understand that the remedy for the loneliness that drives us almost to suicide, is hidden in that bag. We have left behind in that bag: prayer, faith, love, hope, all things that used to make a person whole. All have gone. Unless we find that bag it will be most tragic because loneliness will envelop us with its immense, unrelenting mantle. It will cover us, and although we be yet alive, we will be buried in its grave—the grave of loneliness, where one does not really hear, or speak, or understand. The black mantle of loneliness is building a grave on top of us.

But, as I said, we are discussing you and me. What about us? About us, it is very simple: we have lost the ability to laugh, to enjoy ourselves. We have lost the joy of the simple things which were so good. The evenings with father and mother when little children were told fairy tales and went to sleep dreaming of beautiful ladies and the like. It was a time when little farms dotted the land and most men were farmers. It was the time when children learned about trees and flowers, wheat, oats and how they grew; when little fellows with little rakes tried to help their fathers in saving the hay, and there was fun for everybody.

There were the church suppers too, where everyone was friendly, and everyone knew each other in the little villages and towns. There were the barn dances, the thousand things that seem old but could become new any day because they are immortal, and they disperse loneliness like wind disperses a fog. When people communicate, loneliness is broken into tiny pieces that are scattered by the wind.

Communication is the enemy of loneliness. However, to communicate, one has to laugh. Recently I was in a clinic for a check up. I was astonished at the kindness and constancy of all—patients, personnel, doctors, nurses. The clinic had been built with love, sympathy, and understanding of the sick. I thought to myself: this is what disperses loneliness. There were so many lonely people in that clinic, and communication lifted it. Just a little word or a smile, a helping hand here or there, a little conversation while waiting, all these little things meant much to many people. How simple the ways of God are, how very simple!

Christ, who experienced the greatest loneliness in a manner of speaking, gives us the power to communicate simple gestures of love: a smile, a helping hand. . . . It is he who directs us to communicate.

Meditation 3

In the last meditation we discussed various types of loneliness and loneliness in general; but now we have to face a little bit more of what we call loneliness. Like Dante's circles of hell, purgatory and heaven, so we too have to view loneliness as rings within our soul, for there are many.

Loneliness has many rings or circles, and at times we live in one circle, never wishing to get out of it. It is a peaceful circle, a ring. We are the "Hi, how are you?" type of person. We realize, though, that each word that we say is totally superficial and does not communicate anything to anybody. This is a circle in which man returns constantly to the point which he left. It is livable. One can go through life with shallow greetings and senseless questions, but when one tries to love these people, the "Hi" interferes. This person does not want to shed his or her loneliness, nor reveal themselves. They do not desire to communicate even with the people with whom they are in love or who love them.

So they trudge a strange circle that I would call a purgatory. It isn't a true purgatory, but it is most difficult to eternally communicate superficially, to have no friend with whom we can talk or share. Such a circle is hard on people for it is a non-sharing circle or ring. Even to the best loved people, the heart is not opened, and others are not loved in the way that Christ expects others to be loved selflessly. Always we approach that circle, for we constantly move around to meet ourselves and start from the same point again and again.

Despair is building up; it is not yet complete despair—that may come later. Still, it is rather close to what it will be tomorrow or the day after. It is a place where feelingless greetings run shallow. Communication is really non-existent. It may be better than nothing at all but it is really tragic just the same for, in the midst of the words that we utter, loneliness laughs at us. If loneliness could speak it would say, "You are my own. You will not escape, for you do not know how to share and communicate."

When sleep is not possible in the night, for an hour or two, loneliness penetrates it like lightning. Then suddenly you see the sun after the storm. You look up, and at that moment you understand what it is you could be if only you overcame the lack of loving. For, believe it or not, the reason why we speak so superficially is because we are hiding ourselves from people. We do not wish them to have a part in us. We want to be alone, and yet we desperately desire friendship and understanding. Thus, loneliness holds us tight, and Dante's ring moves between hell and purgatory.

There are moments in the depths of night when we see, for a second, the sun shining brightly on everything, and beckoning us to come and warm ourselves in its rays. It calls us. It says, "Come! Become human. Cease to be alone. Begin to love. Begin to get involved with others. Begin to love your neighbor." Suddenly, you understand that it is the Son who is talking to you; it is God who is calling you to get out of the morass of your loneliness. "Reach out and touch someone," says the ad. Touch someone with the speech of your lips. Break the loneliness of others, and you will never be lonely again.

Did you ever go into the nursing homes for senior citizens? There are whole floors of lonely people. Do something about it. Do something for others. I recall one time I was in a subway in Montreal. I was reading a book when the lady across from me, who was elderly, looked at me and said, "You have a kind face. Would you mind talking to me a little? I have had the flu for the last three weeks and only a nurse visited me for half an hour. The landlady would bring me a tray, but neither of them spoke very much. It seems I am hungry for human speech; I am hungry to share with someone. That is the way I feel."

We made two trips on the subway from one end to another. Then I invited her to a coffee shop and we became good friends. I did not live in Montreal but we corresponded until she died. I hope, in fact I know, that her loneliness had disappeared because there was someone on the other end. There was an ear that listened lovingly. That is all we have to do.

But as I said, loneliness has many levels. You can go from one to another. You can end in a depression, for loneliness is one of the reasons for emotionally induced diseases. People leap off bridges because of loneliness, and die in nursing homes because they have been neglected by everyone whom they loved. Did you ever watch the women who look through garbage cans? I wish that some photographer would take their picture and make an exhibit in a big city. They walk with their shopping bags, collecting the remnants. A series of those pictures would let us know that we have come close to an insanity created by the complete egotism and indifference of people. For these are the ones that we must go to first. It seems strange that there is a discussion going on politically between "butter and bullets." It is not a question of "butter and bullets"; it is a question of "bread and bullets." Factually, there would be no question about bullets if the world believed in the teaching of Christ: "Love your God, love your neighbor, and love your enemies."

There are three wide, beautiful roads to killing loneliness. Moreover, loneliness should be killed. If our society is geared exclusively for profit, and we give of our surplus only, we are not in tune with Christ's teachings. First and foremost, we must give ourselves, never mind our money. This we might have to give too, but it should be so given that the lonely benefit by it.

At the present moment, huge churches seem to spring up all over. But, as Mother Teresa of Calcutta said when she refused the dinner which accompanies the Nobel Prize winner at a cost of several thousand dollars, "Use this money for the poor." All those cults and strange ways of worshipping seem to concentrate predominantly on themselves. Yes, it is wonderful to be cured, and to pray in a beautiful church, but perhaps we should build less beautiful churches so that the poor might benefit by the money that is given to the church.

God dwelt in a tent in the Old Testament, and Solomon was the first to build him a rich house. But Christ, the Son of God, reverted back to the tent. He who supped with the poor, who healed prostitutes and robbers, did not seem to wish to have anything better than a small little synagogue in which he prayed. True, he went to the temple of Solomon, but more often, he prayed to his Father in the open, on the hillsides and on the mountains.

What I am trying to say is that because loneliness has many levels, many rings, many circles, one can slip deep down and become a patient in a mental institution, or one can also ascend, and overcome the superficiality. One can really stop and look at his neighbor whoever he is, straight in the eye, and say, "Friend, how are you? Tell me about yourself."

Perhaps that is why Madonna House has inaugurated listening houses. You would be very surprised—or would you?—to learn that many people come to our Ottawa house, just to talk. It seems there is no one else in the capital of Canada who listens.

Meditation 4

We discussed communications. We agreed that the only remedy against loneliness is communication, to touch someone, not only physically, but gladly, joyfully, simply, in a friendly fashion. It is quite easy, you know, if you really love people. But you have to love your brothers and sisters, and love them as they are, not expecting from them some performance, or something extraordinary. You have to take them as they are, like the people on the street, or the friends that you have. You have to accept those who call themselves your friends, and even your enemies.

One of the ways of dealing with loneliness, and dealing it a hard blow, is acceptance of people as they are. Then friendliness toward my brother and sister becomes quite normal and natural, and I can communicate with them on the level at which they are.

Really, we have two ways of dealing with loneliness. For when we enter the field of communication, we enter into the field of sanctity. Communication incarnates the words of Christ that we should love one another as he has loved us. When we enter the field of communication, we enter a deep and profound mystery.

One cannot truly communicate with the other except with the help of God. And so one must pray to the Holy Spirit, and, strangely enough, to the woman who was wrapped in silence—Mary. She did not communicate orally, but her benedictions, her way of communicating, were truly miraculous because her love was almost infinite. That is why she could communicate with kings and with the lowly, if they allowed her to. Of course, if people put up walls between the Holy Spirit, or her, and themselves, then there was no communication.

But I want to make this quite clear: to communicate truly with another can only be done through prayer, and powerful prayer. For this means that one loves the person with whom he or she communicates, and this love is of God. The Triune God can lift us to the immense heights that are required to love another as he has loved us. No fear should be attached to this act, this state of loving; if through your parents and others, you have been exposed to true Christianity, then it will be easier.

And so, fundamentally, communication is prayer; this is difficult for people to understand. To span the distance between the casual greeting and the realm of deep, earnest, and loving prayer to him who is Love, is not very easy, but it has to be done. For we cannot communicate unless we love.

Also, to communicate one must hope as well as love; and one must sit under the tree of faith. Otherwise all communiction will be false and will ring falsely as sham in the ears of him with whom we try to communicate, and he will not respond. If communication is really to move the heart of the person with whom we try to communicate, there must be complete simplicity. Then something happens to that other person. Suddenly, strange as it might seem, they look at us, and in our humble features, they see the face of him who died for love of them. And because they see, they catch a glimpse of something, and their heart opens, and we can communicate with them. Now the fulfillment of Christ's desire of the new commandment that he gave us, to love one another, and to love our enemies, comes to full flower, and the world is renewed once more, because the Lord truly smiles upon it.

Meditation 5

We have considered loneliness quite a bit, but there is always more to consider. We have mentioned that loneliness is a state, an emotion, that it can come from the depths of hell, but then again it can come from the heights of heaven.

One of the first things in facing loneliness, especially old age loneliness, or any kind of loneliness, is to understand that Christ calls some people to share his loneliness. This calling is redemptive. For if we share the loneliness of Christ, then we too, with his help, can redeem the world. All those who follow in his footsteps, all those who never deviate from his teachings, find that these teachings are revolutionary.

In fact, no revolutionary wants to accept them. Revolutionaries want to do what they want to do, when they want to do it and as they want to do it, but they do not want to do what Christ told them to do. Hence, there is no peace in the world. But those who follow Christ will find peace, and will understand that loneliness is fruitful and not sterile, because we can share it, if we wish to, with God.

I had a psychiatrist friend who used to tell me that whenever I had those come to ask my advice about loneliness, I should take them by the hand and lead them to Gethsemani . . . to the utter loneliness of Christ as the Apostles slept. There they could see Christ in his loneliness sweating blood upon a stone and thereby, in a manner of speaking, gathering up the loneliness of the whole world as his precious blood fell upon the stone. Incidentally, that is why stones are precious. Ordinary stones, in the eyes of the beholder who believes, are impregnated with drops of his precious blood. Sometimes, if you touch a stone, even a little pebble, loneliness disappears—if you have faith.

There is another point which has to be investigated when we discuss loneliness. If we wish to get rid of loneliness, we have to make contact with God, through prayer. But, there is an even deeper contact than prayer. Prayers of petition, and the like, are wonderful, but when we want to get rid of loneliness, we have to come closer and enter the mystery of Christ's loneliness. We must enter it without understanding it, as it is impossible to understand; so, we have to make contact with God.

Consider. The entry into God's mysteries with the key of prayer brings us to the periphery of the sobrania* of God the Father, Son and Holy Spirit. This was the original sobrania, the

* A Russian word meaning "unity."

original unity. So we come to the periphery of this unity, and are practically in it; thus, we make a contact with it. Having made this contact, the contact with men, with my brothers and my sisters, comes naturally. My heart and your heart are so inflamed with love, that they go through the world shedding love, bringing love, and putting the world on fire. Yes, that will eliminate loneliness from the lives of our brothers and sisters everywhere—and from us, too. If we truly enter God's mystery, even at its periphery, we must love him. To him who loves God, the world is a toy to play with, together with the Christ-Child.

Meditation 6

We have discussed the remedies for loneliness. The first remedy is contact with God; that is to say, not only a contact but an incarnation into the Lord. This incarnation is found when two people love one another.

It is obvious that God has passionately loved us, or he would not have died on the cross. The question remains, do we passionately love him? It is not enough to just be in contact with God. There is still a great difference between simple contact with God, and being passionately in love with him in such a manner that the Gospel and all his words become our guidelines. These are the only guidelines that we acknowledge, because love is like that. Those who love one another march to one tune and no other.

Once this love affair between God and us, and especially between the Second Person and us has been established, God will be there to help us, to confront us. We must have a real confrontation with God. He strips us bare. There is nothing left of us except the naked soul, totally open to God. He can throw away the keys to such a soul, because the doors are open most of the time. This is because everyone who walks into such a soul, into such a heart, is the Lord, is Christ.

Mother Teresa of Calcutta understands that, and in a book entitled *Something Beautiful for God*, Malcomb Muggeridge writes about it. But, it is one thing to write about someone, and it is another thing to experience what that someone lives. I have not met Mother Teresa; I have only corresponded with her once or twice. But I think that she and I know each other because we are both in love with God in a deep way. It is hard to describe this state of loving God, for all words become useless.

In a book which I wrote entitled *Molchanie* —meaning "silence" in Russian—I tried to explain that when one enters the mystery of God, the first mystery is silence. When one loves another, silence is absolutely necessary.

Long before lovers can speak openly of their love, they speak by silence, a deep silence, especially when it deals with God. It is by entering the mystery of silence that slowly everyone becomes like our Beloved. That is true of Mother Teresa. Hers is a very heroic quality. Once that mystery is embraced no words are needed to describe heroism, sanctity, or things of that nature. For everything which we do for the other, my brothers and sisters, is done for him.

Can you really imagine joy; pure, unadulterated joy? Well, cup your hands and let joy become bread and wine in your hands. Open your mouth, take it, and swallow it. Receive communion. Become one with God, and at that very moment a very great mystery takes place. In this communion you will see each face of your brothers and sisters as the face of God.

Meditation 7

We are still considering the mystery of loneliness. The question is: Can anyone probe mysteries? This kind of mystery belongs to God. When we say "mystery," the result is obvious. We walk on the periphery of that mystery, but we cannot enter it—unless, of course, God permits us to. Sometimes he does, and when he does, hold it in your cupped hands. He has allowed you to penetrate the mystery of his own mystery of loneliness.

Have you ever considered how lonely Christ was? What he felt as he entered the womb of his creature? A fantastic loneliness overcame a foetus. Can you, for one second, understand the immense, infinite, the absolutely incredible love of the Father, Son, and Holy Spirit? This is the first of the mysteries. It is not only a love letter that God has written to you and to me, but it is an explosion of love.

We read today of volcanoes which explode. We worry about the explosion of nuclear weapons, but here within your heart, if you let it be open, is the greatest explosion of all: the explosion of the love of God for men which goes to the length of becoming a seed in the womb of a woman. Can we understand that fully? One thing we can do: we can fall on our knees, and prostrate ourselves before the incredible mystery of his love.

We can continue to meditate on the mysteries, for they are there to be meditated on, as in the Rosary. You hold it in your hand and you move one bead to another bead. It is the love of God for you and me. And as you keep passing those beads through your fingers, they become more than beads. They are something very real because they deal with his mysteries.

In a book that I have written called *Sobornost*, I attempted to describe the unity of God and man. God looked at what he had created and he decided that he would make man like unto himself. God wanted communication with man; but man did not want to have any communication with God once he had understood the rules of communication. And those rules were rules of love: first the love of God, secondly, people; but man wanted to love himself. So, the apple of pride became bigger, and bigger, and appeared like a little moon somewhere in the sky. Only it wasn't in the sky, it was in the heart of men: in your heart and my heart.

We didn't want to communicate with God. It was too hard. Communication with God meant following the Second Person of the Most Holy Trinity. It meant a sort of station of the Cross. When we heard the sound of nails on flesh, that was immediately one reason why we said to ourselves in the darkness of the night, "Not me, God, not me. I'll take some of it, but not all of it." But with God, if we don't take all of it, he disappears.

The loneliness of the unbeliever comes out of hell and not out of heaven. It takes charge of one. All I can do for whoever you are who reads this book, is pray for you. For the loneliness that comes to you from heaven is the loneliness of the Garden of Gethsemani. The apostles are asleep, but you are not. You touch the rim of another mystery, the mystery of Christ's blood falling on a stone, and his cry in the night to his Father. You are next to him. You are part of that mystery of his loneliness, and because you are part of it, your heart begins to burn with a love that you cannot contain. You forget everything, and wordlessly you begin to communicate with him; then the loneliness vanishes. You are there, at the Crucifixion—and you do not even feel the nails in your hands and feet because love fills your whole person. You are taken out of yourself and you are placed into his heart. Now you know the price that he paid for you and me. You know it totally and completely.

Now he is taken off the Cross; but in three days, he will appear to many. In other words, his resurrection is yours. He resurrected for you and for me. You feel the effect of the Resurrection in yourself. Deep down, the mystery of it is all around you. Suddenly you understand. Like St. Paul, like all the apostles, you cannot contain yourself any more.

Now you have to have contact with everyone: face to face, soul to soul, mind to mind. You begin to touch your brothers and sisters in the world, whoever they are, whether prostitutes or kings. For each of you has a gift. You can give to each the gift of prayer, which is the golden key that God gave you to enter his mysteries. And the greatest mystery of all is that, in communicating with God in depth, you communicate with men in depth. The strangest thing happens. Suddenly, because your eyes have been opened, you now know that each person that you communicate with, is Christ Himself. With his arms wide open, he says, "Come to me all you who labor and are burdened and I will refresh you."

Meditation 8

If we really understood loneliness, we would know without knowing, we would grasp without grasping, we would feel without feeling, just one thing: that my brother is Christ.

This will come to us after awhile. Perhaps one has to go through the poustinia, because in the great desert one can see so clearly the face of God. And in sobrania, which is the unity of the Trinity with me and you, it is obvious that he who sees the Father knows the Son, and that only the Son can teach us the Father. He who knows the Son knows mankind, irrespective of nationality, color, locale. All men become brothers of him Who is my brother.

Then, of course, the Third Person of the Trinity is the Holy Spirit. The Crimson Dove, as the Russians say, with his immense crimson wings, removes all misunderstanding, all darkness. Now in deed and truth, my brother—the yellow, the black, the white man—becomes Christ.

A very strange thing happens. Truly my brother changes into Christ, but what is much more important, Christ becomes my brother. Do you see how everyone who understands this mystery— God teaches it to you—suddenly realize that they are surrounded on all sides by the most Holy Trinity?

Then something happens to loneliness. It ceases to be an illness that I go to the psychiatrist to cure. Why don't you look at your hands, dear reader, and see if perhaps you have in your hands a key? It is a key, a very simple, ordinary key that opens to you the true essence of loneliness, which is *sharing it with Christ*. But if you share it with him, may I ask you, how is it possible to be lonely when you have the key to his loneliness, and the two lonelinesses blend together? Each ceases to be a loneliness, doesn't it?

Now, you might be in Gethsemani where he was so very lonely. Or you might be anywhere: on a street car or a bus, in Ottawa, or Paris, or Berlin on some path leading to a rural area. You can share his loneliness at any time, and he will share yours. The result will be that there will not be any loneliness, because when you have entered into the mystery of Christ's loneliness, it ceases to be loneliness. Now, out of your soul, out of your mind, out of your heart, comes your dance, and your song, and your joy; for fundamentally, dear friends, one entry into the loneliness of Christ is a time of celebration because we have been given the key to one of the greatest mysteries of God.

It will take you time to slowly bring your hands together. When you are lonely, you sort of look "down," and your hands, too, hang "down" at your sides. But very slowly, as you pray, notwithstanding the drooping arms, notwithstanding the head that seems too heavy for you to carry, notwithstanding the back that is breaking under what you think is his cross, slowly, with a deep breath, your hands come together. First, praying hands, then open hands, lifted up to God as if they were a chalice. You can drink water out of your cupped hands. So you lift them, one next to another. If you continue to pray, a strange sound will enter your ears and a key will drop into your hands lifted like a chalice to him. Slowly you will take the key, and it will open his heart. You will step over the threshold because, you see, he only allows us to see the fringe of his mysteries. There are very few who go into the depth of his mysteries. No doubt, our Lady did.

So, using the key, you walk into this mystery. You already know how straight is your back, how raised is your head, and how joyous is your song and dance before him! You hold hands with him, and you go skipping and hopping and jumping with God! Why? Because he has given you the one thing which we all desire but very seldom like to receive: love. It is painful, and takes much prayer and much wandering across unknown places and deserts and hills. Yes, it takes much to love your brother, and therefore to love your God.

Meditation 9

We have been discussing loneliness. And yet, if we think of it, we really have not discussed anything because one cannot discuss loneliness. The only way we could discuss loneliness is if we could enter Christ's loneliness.

For some unaccountable reason, my mind turns toward obedience. Here is God, the Second Person of the Most Holy Trinity. The Father sends him down to redeem us. And, without a murmur, he enters as a seed into a woman's womb. How did he do it? He was God. I know that many heresies arose regarding that point, and many people argued about it. I do not argue, and I am not interested in heresy. I just behold the humility of Christ. I behold the love of Christ, for only lovers can do such things.

Those of us who were baptized in his name are his Body, the people of God. He is our Head. This is good theology. But there is here a tremendous mystery. It is as if I approach slowly, barefoot, towards this mystery, shining in the distance. Then I stop, because it is one of the incomprehensible mysteries. The only way man could understand this mystery, embrace it, is if man loved God as God loved him. Then, and only then, the mystery of the Redemption is revealed. What is the mystery of the Redemption? It is the mystery of the passionate love of God for man.

So then, man must seek to love God the same way that God loves him; this is what Christ said we should do. "A new commandment I give unto you, that you love one another as I have loved you." Thus, we stand in front of this mystery. Suddenly, he takes us by the hand and says, "Come." Then, as we move into this mystery, the mystery of love opens before us, the mystery of surrender to the cross, the mystery of the resurrection.

Too, there is always his passionate love of his Church. True, the Church has other mysteries. True, it is the bride of Christ, and if you want to probe loneliness, that is where you have to enter. You have to penetrate the mystery of Christ becoming man, and then you will know what loneliness is. It will frighten you and you will try to run from it; but stay. Keep moving *into* the mystery. As you move in, as the door of love, the door of surrender, the door of obedience, and the door of passionate loving opens, something will happen to you. Your loneliness will completely change.

I do not care if you have the most beloved husband or wife in the world. It makes no difference if you are a nun, or a priest who is completely lost in love with God. You will always know the incredible longing for the unity of man in God.

At some point, maybe in your youth, maybe in your old age, maybe in your middle age—you will suddenly feel that your lifted hands, which were praying to God and fasting, will slowly come down, and, instead of lying as usual by your side, they will come down, and loneliness will disappear. You cannot even imagine loneliness now because your hands have finally reached the hands of Christ.

Then, there will remain only one thing. He will bend down his face, and, as it says in Song of Songs, he will kiss you on the lips. You will look around, and there will be no loneliness. Death makes loneliness disappear forever. Not only will faith and hope fall away, but loneliness will fall away.

However, we have to live in this world until death comes to fetch us. Now, since God has invited you to come into this mystery of his loneliness, since you have probed it, tasted it, felt it; since your hands and feet have the sign of nails; since you have explored his love for his Church—the Bride—since those things have happened to you, do not think for a moment that they are there just for you. No! They are there for everyone. Now, at long last, your hands are in the hands of Christ. But before your lips touch his, you have to assuage the loneliness of others who have not moved into the mystery of God's loneliness.

Now, you have one great work of God's mercy to perform: Go and assuage loneliness. Make those people who think they are alone understand that no one is ever alone, because everyone is with Christ. Go, for the time is ripe! The whole earth is lonely. Go forth, and chase away the loneliness!

Meditation 10

Loneliness has built a bridge. To everyone who wants to cross it, it promises to disappear. If it has not quite disappeared, it has a smiling face. The bridge that, in fact, dispels loneliness is friendship, and forgiveness.

I cannot be lonely, I can never be lonely, if I forgive. But forgiveness must be total. Man is not capable of totally forgiving, unless he has recourse to God, and it is only through God, and through the grace of God, that we can forgive one another totally.

Now forgiveness of this type is truly love. It penetrates that mystery that God has given us. He said, "Love one another, as I have loved you." He also added, "Love your enemies." Now then, see how forgiveness dispels loneliness.

It is a bridge that is soon left behind, because once one enters loneliness with a heart full of forgiveness toward those who have hurt one, loneliness disappears; it just isn't there, it can't be there. It flies from forgiveness because it is the only remedy that can make it disappear.

Forgiveness and friendship: as I forgive my brothers and sisters, a new bridge arises. It might be a suspension bridge, it might be one of cement, it doesn't matter. It is a bridge of friendship.

Now, because you have forgiven your brothers and sisters, you can become friends with them. To be a friend means to share. It is impossible for loneliness to exist between those who share their thoughts and their actions on the basis of forgiveness and friendship.

But friendship, like forgiveness, must be total. It is a strange thing that, as you approach a mystery of Christ, and even as you stand on the periphery of it, a great light dawns on you. You understand without understanding that Christ demands totality. He really does. He would not give one dollar if he had a hundred. And you, also, have to give totally. Our gifts are ours to give freely. Friendship and forgiveness: They must be total. I cannot turn to you and say, ''You are my friend,'' and yet, hide things from you. I must share.

For you see, all of this together becomes a chalice made by the hands of men for God. That chalice must be pure, and its content must be pure. Friendship must be pure, forgiveness must be pure, and total.

Another thing you must understand if you want to break loneliness is that the totality has to continue until you die. Say that you have made friends with some people and suddenly the shadow of anger, or of unforgiveness, darts through your soul. You hadn't done anything to those people except that you had withdrawn. Now, the loneliness that men are afraid of will come and envelop you in its mantle again. Of course you must understand, as I have tried already to explain, that there is a type of loneliness that has nothing to do with friendship or forgiveness. You will always have one type of loneliness, because your heart will never be satisfied unless it is placed into the heart of God. He reserves this joy for himself.

Even though forgiveness, friendship, understanding, and love, constantly bind us to one another and present to God a joyful picture, nevertheless, in both the dark of the night and in the noonday sun, I turn my face to him and I say, "Lord, notwithstanding all this that You have given me, I am still lonely because as yet I do not possess You totally."

And so, in a certain sense, you will have to remain lonely. But let me tell you, this kind of loneliness is beautiful. It can be likened to the loneliness of a young girl desirous to meet her fiancee. You might be very old, your face wrinkled with age, and your hair gray or white. You might have old shoes or slippers on your feet. You might go with a bag gathering the garbage of others, or you might be wealthy. None of this matters. Whoever you are—men, women, youth—somehow or other you must think of yourself as lifting your hands toward someone and saying, "Oh, I am lonely, because You are not here."

REJECTION

Meditation 1

To reject means not to accept. It is an amazing thing how rejection can hurt beyond any other state or emotion. To be rejected, not to be accepted, is to enter a dark, tragic garden that appears to be all evil. There is nothing about it that appears to be normal. No, it is all surrealistic.

Not to be accepted, to be obviously and definitely rejected by one's own, is for those who love God, to enter into Gethsemani.

Consider, very simply, that Jesus went to Gethsemani to pray. He took a few disciples with him. They were overcome with sleep. He went and knelt by a flat stone, possibly like a table, so that he could put his hands on it. He prayed as only the Son of God, as only Jesus, could pray. A sense of desolation overtook him. He arose, and he went to those who slept. He looked at them and said, ''So you had not the strength to keep awake with me one hour?'' As he turned back from them, the sense of rejection must have been absolutely incredible, because the Son of God felt, that even his Father seemed to reject him. He cried out, ''My Father, if this cup cannot pass by without my drinking it, your will be done!''

These are words which express a sense of total desolation and rejection by man and God.

Again, on the Cross, he would cry out to his Father, ''Abba, Abba, why have you forsaken Me?''

Now stop right here and try, if you can, by prayer, by identification, by every means at your disposal, to identify yourself with the desolate, rejected Christ.

The Garden of Gethsemani is the place where you can share that rejection, and you can say to God—at least I do—''Lord, I am not asleep. I am praying with you right by this stone. I do not reject you. On the contrary, my heart accepts you as the greatest gift that your Father has given us.'' I do not know if that will console him. But each person, each believer, must speak for himself. This kind of prayer cannot be taught.

When he was led to Golgotha under the weight of his cross, people mocked him. When he was crucified, they continued mocking him, and they said, ''He saved others; he cannot save himself.

He is the king of Israel: let him come down from the cross now, and we will believe in him.'' In the mob that surrounded him, he saw hundreds of people whom his gentleness and kindness had cured, and on whom he had lavished his miracles of love. The people to whom he had said, ''Your faith has made you whole,'' were there also. They rejected him, as if he indeed was the criminal whom the Romans and the Jews said he was. Crucifixion was a shameful end to a shameful career. So, the Second Person of the Most Holy Trinity died between two thieves.

The rejection seemed complete. How profound, how deep, how lasting were the wounds of that rejection! A little group of women, and St. John the beloved apostle, stood beneath the cross. But the hardest rejection for him must have been the fact that the rest of his disciples vanished. Perhaps he could see them from the height of his cross. Perhaps he could see the dust that their bare feet or sandals made as they ran away.

Let us pause for a moment and enter the bitter depths of that rejection, standing side by side with him unto the end, preaching the gospel without compromise, with your very body, mind, heart, and soul, and crying out within, ''Lord, I throw my life at your feet and sing, that I can bring You such a small thing.'' At that moment we suddenly shall know the joy of rejection.

Meditation 2

Long before Jesus went to Gethsemani and stumbled under the weight of the cross, an unassuming young woman was going about her business. Suddenly an angel appeared to her, and prostrating himself before her, he announced to her that she was chosen by God to bear his Son. The angel said, ''Hail, full of grace, the Lord is with you,'' the introduction to the prayer that today is known across the world.

Although she was fifteen years old or thereabouts, she was the Mother of Wisdom, even if she did not know it at the moment. She had discernment, and she simply said, ''How will it be possible, for I know not man?'' The angel explained to her that the Holy

Spirit would overshadow her, and that he who would be born from her would be the Son of the Most High. She listened to all this, and then became the example of perfect acceptance of the will of God.

She listened and she said, "I am the handmaid of the Lord, let what you have said be done to me." That was full acceptance. But rejection followed almost at once after the disappearance of the angel. As soon as her pregnancy became evident, Joseph, to whom she was engaged, rejected her in his mind in a strange manner. He could not quite understand, and he wondered. There were moments when he wanted to divorce her. This was a form of rejection.

And so even before her child was born, she felt the whip of rejection. Joseph could have accused her of adultery; but she never said one single word to Joseph to justify herself.

In a sense, her feeling of rejection must have been very complete. Before the Son was born, the mother partook of the bitter chalice of rejection and drank it without saying a word in her defense.

Then, Joseph had a dream and he married her. Still, she had walked alone for so long. It was the dream that revealed to Joseph what the facts were. The point is that he permitted himself to be born in a set of strange, unexplicable circumstances which were a suffering for his mother.

Let us not forget Mary. After Christ's birth, she first experienced a great consolation: the coming of the Magi. But she was barely able to absorb the joy of the visit, and the joy of her son being born, when rejection overtook her once again: Herod decided to kill all children of the age of her son. Again, in a dream, Joseph was told to take her and the child to Egypt. Her own people rejected her. Did you ever stop and think that Mary is the Queen of the refugees?

What happens to refugees? They pass through a terrible experience. They feel as though both nations have rejected them.

I suppose that she finally was happy when she returned, and led an ordinary life of a wife and a mother. But all the time there was a mystery around her, and I feel that the people of Nazareth sensed it.

Later, she suffered another rejection. After Cana she went to see Jesus. Suddenly her son stood up and said, "Who is my mother? Who are my brothers? Anyone who does the will of my Father in heaven, he is my brother and sister and mother." How did she feel? True, she understood the spiritual significance of the teaching. But, nonetheless, humanly speaking, that seeming rejection must have been hard to bear. Although it was said gently, she was still his mother.

Another time the Sanhedrin rejected him: "Who is he? He is the son of a carpenter. He is a Nazarene. Nothing good comes from Nazareth." This rejection of Jesus was rejection for Mary.

Mary was truly a marvelous person, sensitive beyond all normal human sensitivity. She was the Seat of Wisdom. How did she make it through "the way of the cross," when Christ carried his cross to Golgotha? She watched him fall; she watched his beaten body; she saw that face that had been so dear to her covered with the mud and the dust of the Holy Land. Just as Simeon had predicted, she felt the sword going through her heart. As Jesus fell down amid the jeers and rejection of the people, she was there. She united herself with him. They were always united. What he felt, she felt, for was not she his mother and did not she, beyond all others, understand who he really was?

When the ordeal was over, they laid him in her arms; she held him fast. I looked hard and long at the Pieta in Rome. How profound was her feeling. Both he and she were rejected by the mob, by those he had cured and helped. But she remembered the words he had said to St. John and herself. As she held him in her arms she must have foreseen, with the wisdom that was hers, the bitter rejection that would come to her son and to herself down through the centuries.

He had asked her to be the mother of men. But was she accepted? How many of us accept her? How many of us accept her Son? For us, she exists solely to point out to us the way that leads to her Son, but no arms are stretched out to accept her Son. All kinds of ideas are rampant even among the baptized. Some do not truly accept Christ. How bitter is that rejection. Ask them!

Meditation 3

I have a couple who write tragic letters to me. They have been rejected by their community. They are wandering like pilgrims, trying to find a place to stay.

Often, we cannot understand why we or others are rejected. It is so simple. We are rejected because God loves us, Mary loves us. Jesus and Mary loves us so much that Jesus wants us to share in his passion, for his passion is his supreme rejection.

If we enter into his Passion, and are ready to be crucified with the nails of rejection which hurt so much, we will know the joy of Christ. We can make up what is lacking in the sufferings of Christ—do we remember that? Do we know that when we are in pain—physical, psychological, spiritual—we are capable of understanding why this pain was given to us. Then we lift our pains (and the pain of rejection is the hardest) into his cupped hands. It is like the water that is added to the wine in the Sacrament of the Eucharist. The Lord takes our pain, especially the pain of rejection, and he uses it to help others across the whole earth.

Yes, it is very hard to understand. I wrote a book called *Fragments of My Life.* In it I touched upon some of my feelings of rejection by certain Christians in both the United States and Canada.

I would like to present a poem I wrote about rejection.

REJECTION

Pain is a
Vivid flame
That enters
The soul
Like a sharp
Sword. . . .

I felt
The sword,
Beheld
The wound,
Saw the red
Of my own
Blood.
Crimson
My heart . . .
As it gushed
From my soul. . . .

The pain
Was searing.
I stood before
My own
Who did not
Want me,
Stood alone
Rejected . . .
Ejected. . . .

I looked around—
In truth
Saw thousands:
Eyes—hands
Piercing
Me through,
Clawing
At me
Viciously. . . .

Someone
Took up
The stones
Of lying
Words

With edges
Sharp—
Threw them
Hard. . . .

They hit
My face
And blinded me.
I fell
And lay
Like one
Dead. . . .

I knew myself
For what
I was:
The rejected
Stone,
Unwanted
By my own. . . .

Now—
the dusty
Road
Is my
Bedding
Place.
On it
I lay
My bleeding
Face. . . .

The dust
Is soft
And dry
And it
Alone

Sings
A lullaby
To a rejected
Stone. . . .

I could say more, but I won't. This year, 1980, was the 50th anniversary of Friendship House and Madonna House. They have been built upon my rejection.

To persevere under the constant blows of a whip of rejection can only be done when Christ and Mary are at your side. Faith alone can continue amid this immolation. The years of rejection follow one after the other like huge stones that are tied about my body. They seem to bring me to the bottom of lakes and rivers. But always, my hands are in the hands of God, of Jesus and Mary. No amount of stones tied around my waist can submerge me.

Having experienced a terrible rejection by many Christians in both Canada and America, I, too, now know the joy that the acceptance of pain brings.

In Canada, I was rejected by some laity and some priests and nuns, but never by the Bishops. I was rejected by my own staff in Harlem. A holy Capuchin once said to me, "Catherine, you are getting there. First you were rejected by the outsiders; now you have been rejected by your own. This is the test that God gives to foundresses." I turned to him, tears running down my face, and blurted out "Oh, what a terrible thing! Who gives one that sort of thing?" Calmly, he told me, "God does, Catherine." I was really numb in those days.

But there was another woman who could have cried out just as I did, "Out of the depths we cry to Thee, O Lord. Hear the voice of our supplications." That was Dorothy Day. What that woman suffered in the way of rejection is beyond any ability of mine to put into words. Constantly she was rejected by everybody. But she learned the secret of rejection before I did. She was serene and peaceful under blows of that rejection. By the way she accepted rejection, she truly taught me as no one has ever taught me. Dorothy Day and Peter Maurin were the shining lights of the 1930's to whom youth came in thousands to learn the secret of accepting rejections. When she became a pacifist during the war, all her houses dwindled; her rejection was almost complete. She was crucified in the marketplace. I learned much from Dorothy Day.

Really, we all can say that we know what rejection is. We know because at one time or another we have all experienced it in our body and in our mind; but we also know and have experienced the tremendous joy of those who follow Christ on the Cross.

Meditation 4

"Father, Father why have you forsaken me?" Those words are filled with mystery and awe. How is it possible that Christ, the Son of the Father, could say such tragic things on the cross? And before that, in Gethsemani, when he begged that the chalice pass him by? How? To me it seems obvious why; but then I have not studied much theology. But I pray. So, to my mind, it appears very simple.

Christ was a man like us in all things except sin. Like any human being, he cried because he was hurting. He said to his Father, "I have really done everything that You wanted Me to do." But this humanity asserted itself.

I am not a theologian, so I beg the pardon of such who may read this book. I would say that in a moment of stress, his humanity engulfed his divinity. He obviously experienced the darkness which we all experience.

We experience our darkness for his sake. The darkness comes to us, and we cry to the same Father, "Father, Father, why have you forsaken me?"

The tragedies of mankind are many. Let us take, for instance, the "boat people" who are Christians. Couldn't they cry out to the Father, "Father, why have You forsaken me?" I think they could.

I think of myself, too, after I left Russia. I have narrated how once when I was on the Brooklyn Bridge, I wanted to jump because my life had become meaningless. I held onto the parapet and I cried, "Father, Father, why have you forsaken me?" My husband was in the hospital. My child was in the home of a stranger. I was earning seven dollars a week. How could I not have cried out to the Father? To whom should have I cried? Only the Father! Underneath the cross of Christ was a sea of people, going back and forth. Many had come just to see him dying. The torture of criminals was like a sports event in those days. From his cross, Christ could see that some of those people were the ones he cured. Imagine the tremendous pain of rejection that overtook him at the sight of those he had helped. It pierced through his soul like a sword. Not only Mary had a sword through her soul, so did he. He turned his head a little, and what did he see. Of his apostles he saw nothing except the dust that they had kicked up in the wake of their flight. Only St. John remained. Could Christ feel anything else but rejection?

The very people he had cured rejected him. The apostles rejected him. People yelled from below, "If you are the Son of God, get down from the cross and we will believe in you." This was blasphemy, of course. Obviously, there was something to cry about to his Father. And he did. In that tremendous cry of Christ from the Cross, the whole of mankind's pain was found.

Karl Stern used to say to me, "When you deal with emotionally depressed people, try to show them how to unite their depression with the depression of God in Gethsemani."

Jesus arose after prayer and came to his disciples, and they were sound asleep. How would you feel about that? Suppose your friends were asleep when you were in a depression, or a terrible bind. He said, "Could you not watch one hour with me?"

So it is not astonishing that Jesus Christ cried out. In his cry we take courage because his cry lifts us up to himself. And the Father listens to our cry as he listened to the cry of his Son. That Son died, but three days later he arose. Thus the Father showed how much he loved his Son. It is the same for us.

When we are so absolutely down, we cry, "Father, Father, why have you forsaken me?" The echo of our voice is in our ears.

This echo is something that moves us up the mountain of the Lord very quickly. The Lord stands on the mountain and says, "Friend, come higher," and we are crying to his Father, "Why have you forsaken me?" But if in total trust, and utter faith, hope, and love, we really bend close to the ground, and continue to appeal to the Father, our voice becomes lower and lower until it becomes a whisper, until we are silent. As we move up the mountain of the Lord we suddenly understand what is happening to us: We are entering into the resurrection of Christ.

Meditation 5

In the last meditation we slowly came to the conclusion that Christ was seemingly rejected by the Father because, being man as well as God, he accepted the sense of rejection experienced by every human being. For every human being deeply feels the rejection of his or her fellow man, and quite often imagines that he or she is also rejected by God.

Inasmuch as Christ was true man and true God, he felt rejection also. At least, that is my idea of the meaning of his cry on the Cross.

There was a psychiatrist named Jung, who was a pupil of Freud, but who eventually separated from him. Jung made a tour of the world, analyzing nations and peoples. When he finished he returned home, and wrote up his findings. He concluded that all men feel rejected by God. He found that there was a deep rift at the bottom of men's souls, between themselves and that Someone greater than themselves.

Rejection often stems from imaginary or real guilt. Various people tend to act differently when faced with rejection. The English, it is said, enclose themselves in their so-called unemotional cape; while the French verbalize. Those who verbalize are often cured from imaginary rejection.

For instance, let us consider mortal sin which today is not spoken of at all. Mortal sin is an offense toward God, and the guilt of it, if it is not verbalized (confessed), is like a cancer eating up one's heart and soul. It is hard to visualize the heart and soul being eaten up by cancer; yet, when it happens, it upsets the equilibrium of the entire person. Or again, to feel guilt when there is no reason for guilt is a terrible thing. It is better to feel guilty when there is some reason for guilt; then at least one can go and verbalize to a priest, or anyone whom you feel is worthy of your verbalization.

The answer to this terrible state of affairs is to share what is in your soul, your heart, with someone else.

Obviously one should be sharing it with Christ or the Trinity, or with our Lady, or with the saints, but this is a little too esoteric for our modern century. We have to share with a human being. We remember that Christ walked the earth. Step by step, walking with him, believing that he is the first person in whom we should confide, we walk with him in faith and in trust, and we tell him our problems. But inasmuch as we are human, it seems that we require a human being to confide in, and to talk to. This is called friendship, holy friendship; it leads the other to God. Thus, each being is able to discuss himself or herself to the very depths with the other. If this is not done, the body and soul are poisoned with the eternal poisoning of guilt.

So, strange as this might seem, guilt and rejection are almost twin sisters. It appears that one has to go to a surgeon to have guilt removed. The surgeon is the priest. He must assuage the guilt. He must allow it to die, slowly but surely, so that the human person can proceed and be receptive to rejection. For when one receives rejection in its pure form, it means one is accepting that rejection which Christ accepted. The fact that my friends are sleeping while I pray and am in an agony does not affect me. The fact that people are calling me names, causes me to dance. Why? Because Christ was called names: worse ones than I will ever be called.

Thus rejection accepted in faith is acceptance by Christ. Did you ever think about that? If you accept rejection because you love God, a strange thing happens. God comes down to you—into you—and you begin to feel as if you are walking on air. Why? Because you chose something much more powerful: your rejection with Christ's rejection. In the fusing of the two you walk directly into the resurrected Christ. In the resurrected Christ, you care little about any rejection. It becomes joy, not sorrow. If you feel a twinge of guilt, you say, "Go away, for I know the resurrected Christ. I am one with that rejection experienced by God."

God the Father says, "I have not rejected you. I have loved you from time immemorial. I have created you out of nothing, and you are mine. I have made you what you are. I, God the Father, shaped you. God the Son died for you. God the Holy Spirit overshadowed you. No, you are not rejected. You are the friend of my Son, filled with peace and joy. If you have faith, rejection will lie at your feet and then disappear. I will never reject you. Therefore, be at peace.'' Your face reflects the face of my Son, as well as mine. Rejection is a lie of the devil.

Meditation 6

This meditation deals with rejection of a particular sort, a basic kind of rejection so rampant in the world today: childhood rejection. This form of rejection begins in the womb of the mother: the unwanted baby, whom the mother carries because she has to, not because she wants to, not because she loves the child.

I am not a psychiatrist, but I know that even the unborn child somehow feels the rejection by its mother.

Then comes birth, which for the baby usually is a traumatic experience because the child dislikes leaving the warm surroundings in which he or she has resided up to then. The sound of a baby that has just been born is always, it seems, almost a sound of anger.

It is this anger that the parents must assuage. Did you ever consider the difference between bottle-fed babies and breast-fed babies? One might object: But the child does not know the difference. Perhaps, but it is a fact that a child who is breast-fed is more peaceful, more quiet, and less subject to feelings of rejection. His anger is assuaged and forgotten because to hold and breast-feed the child, the mother has to cradle him in her arms. A child who is cradled in his mother's arms knows love, or shall we say that, because of those encircling arms, the child does not know rejection.

In Russia, in the old days, and perhaps even today, if the mother could not herself provide the milk for her baby, instead of bottle feeding it, she asked a nursing mother to give suck to her baby. It was important for her that her baby be cradled in loving arms, and suck love through the breasts of a woman. Thence came love.

Yes, but suppose a baby is bottle-fed, and no arms cradle him. He is given a bottle in bed, or in a carriage or stroller. At one time or another he will feel some kind of rejection in this action. Even God felt it through that child. God made woman to feed their babies and not to hand them bottles. Yes, God feels it too.

And then a child begins to grow. . . . In our age of divorces, and of "shacking up," how does a child feel? I talked to one such child. He was about nine years old. I was sitting on the porch of Madonna House when he came along; he sat down by my side, and he began talking. He said, "I like it here." I asked, "Why?" He said, "Everyone is so kind to me. I feel very happy here." I said, "That's nice." He looked at me with big blue eyes and said, "I don't feel happy at home." I asked "Why not?" He said, "Well, here everyone notices me, but at home nobody does. I'm just nobody. My mother seems to look through me. She is nice. She feeds me breakfast, but lunch I get at the school. When I come home there is a woman who gives me some snacks; milk, cookies; but Mommie is never home. She has a job, and she is always away, always away. She is never there. She is home on Sunday, but she and my father quarrel a lot on Sunday. Then they send me to Sunday school. It is all upside down. Everybody here talks about Jesus Christ, but at home nobody does." His language was less stilted than mine. His words were simple. Then he put his head on my knees and began to cry. "Can I stay with you forever? I would be so happy here." But of course he could not. As I watched the car with him and his parents leaving our yard, I said to myself, "Those parents are laying the groundwork of rejection. By the time he is fifteen, there will be a powerful explosion that will shatter his whole life."

Somehow or other, that little boy made me think; and as I thought I went to our little chapel to pray.

A strange thing happened to me. I entered into the depths of rejection, a very difficult thing to explain. I saw it as a number of caves along the seashore. Many children were being put into those caves while the parents went to work. In the caves, something happened. The children were seemingly fed and clothed, but fundamentally I saw they were deprived of love. I saw the ugly face of rejection, and it cried in the night.

Soon I was overwhelmed by the sobbing of children. I no longer saw the caves nor the sea. I just heard sobs, all across the world. Children rejected, children working many hours, children sold into slavery, children sold to pornography, children everywhere. The next thing I knew I was sobbing too. For as I looked into the face of rejection, what else could I do? People did not understand that they were rejecting God; for "whatever you do to one of these little ones, you do it to me."

It seemed that I suddenly heard the voice of God. Did you ever hear, through the Gospel, the voice of Christ? "But anyone who is an obstacle to bring down one of these little ones who have faith in me would be better drowned in the depths of the sea with a great millstone round his neck. Alas for the world that there should be such obstacles! Obstacles indeed there must be, but alas for the man who provides them!" (Mt 18:6) Can you imagine that? He said it *solemnly*—it was no joke. But how many have been rejected!

Everything that we are reaping today—violence, hatred, anger, vandalism, amongst the young—goes back to that strange collective sobbing of children. They don't let anyone know about it, but those of us who love them, hear the sobbing and we sob with them. Those of us who understand, prostrate ourselves before God and cry for mercy.

Meditation 7

Rejection is an immense mystery, one of the many that God places before us. But like all the other mysteries, there is a door and and there is a handle; in due time we are invited to open that door, and enter into that mystery.

Sometimes it takes many years before we face rejection. It may come to us in childhood. Sometimes it comes to us in very early years, or during adolescence. It may come in middle age or in old age.

It is a strange mystery. It is not an easy one to apprehend or comprehend. In fact, one is quite incapable of either apprehending or comprehending it. It has to be entered into. The door must be opened, and we must cross its threshold. Then we must allow ourselves to follow the intricate paths of its roads which sometimes are very wide and straight, and sometimes twisted and complicated.

However, sooner or later we must face at least the edge of that mystery. The first realization which will hit us hard is that we have entered the rejection of Christ! That is why it is a mystery: because he entered it, he lived it, he experienced it. Anything that God experienced is a very great mystery for all mankind and for each one personally. It is his grace alone that allows us to open that door, to cross the threshold, and to face rejection side by side with Christ.

Let's face it. He who has been given the grace to follow Christ, he who has understood that his heart is in love with God, and that he has to follow him no matter where he goes, even into the immense mystery of rejection, will find that it will not be easy.

Christ entered that mystery at an early age. His foster father and his mother who were seeking him when he was preaching in the Temple at twelve years of age, did not understand when he told them that "he was about His Father's business." They did not really reject him, but their very misunderstanding must have been painful to him, because we hunger so much to be understood by our own. However, he never said anything, and was obedient to their wishes until he left his mother's sheltering presence. There is no doubt, that from that very day on, he experienced one rejection after another.

As he was gathering his apostles, they followed him. They could not do otherwise, for he who hears the voice of God so intimately in his heart, rises and follows him. They followed him, yes! But many times, they too, rejected him. Whenever he told them a parable, they wanted it immediately explained. When he spoke to them about "eating his flesh and drinking his blood to have life everlasting," some left him completely. How did he feel?

He was preaching the gospel to the poor, and the poor did not understand, nor did the wealthy. They already were plotting his death. How would you like to walk in the shadow of a death? That is a form of total rejection! Over and over again, he opened his mouth and taught the luminous doctrine of the gospel, and each time his very own did not understand him, and rejected him. The Sadducees, and the Pharisees, the whole Sanhedrin, everyone in power, all mocked him and questioned him. They followed him and listened to him for the sole purpose of rejecting every word that he said! Only the simple, the foolish ones, the "humiliati," the ones who did not seem to matter very much in that society, only they seemed to accept him.

Truly, he had nowhere to lay his head: "Foxes have holes and the birds of the air have nests, but the Son of Man has nowhere to lay his head." And so, as we search, a mystery opens up to us. Somehow a strange light is shining from it. And that which was utterly incomprehensible in the beginning becomes understandable, for we enter the mystery like we enter a body of water. We swim in it. We suddenly are filled with it. It enters into us, and we enter into it, and we know what we have done. Somewhere, someplace, our swimming ceases and we simply are permitted to float. The mystery totally encompasses us and we understand that we have chosen to follow Jesus Christ. We have followed him through his pilgrimages, his wanderings across the Holy Land, and we now know that not only are we rejected by his followers, but also we will face the ultimate rejection. Christ occupied one side of the cross. If we decide to follow him, and taste the bitter cup of rejection, we must be crucified on the other side.

However, long before we are crucified, we will experience that strange feeling of rejection by God the Father. Just like Jesus Christ, we will cry out and say, "Lord, let this chalice pass me by." Or, if we are already crucified, we will cry out into a day suddenly become dark and frightening, "Father, Father why have you forsaken me?" Yes, if we want to know Christ, we must walk with him not only through his childhood, not only through the desert, not only through his years of preaching, but even further. We have to walk at his side, and drink the cup of his total rejection.

Our crucifixion will not be of wood. Rather, it might be of sickness, of desertion by those we love, of death of loved ones, or of a thousand and one things which make up a life. Don't you see, dearly beloved friends, who read this book, that if you really want to follow him, there is only one way: you must enter into the mystery of his rejection. Once you have done so, once you have drunk the bitter cup of rejection, then suddenly you will know a joy that overcomes rejection, that annihilates it as if it were not there. Your face will be lifted toward the face of God, and you will sing because of the joy in your heart. Perhaps you will even dance— who can tell?

Those who follow Christ through Gethsemani and Golgotha also follow him to the Resurrection. Resurrection is a total renewal. We will have followed him to the end, so then we sit by the lake. He will prepare fish and bread for us and we will breakfast with him. Then will our joy be unmarred, and then will we know that in him, through him, with him, we can experience everything that he experienced and come out unscathed.

Meditation 8

Rejection is not as simple as it sometimes appears to be. It is not easy to define. One can easily say that one has been rejected by one's parents, or friends, or associates, and one can say other things to which he or she applies the word rejection. One can understand rejection to mean that he is somewhat shunned, not accepted into the circle of his peers. Many things can be superficially said about rejection.

However, rejection is a profound mystery. It is also a very deep emotion. It is an emotion that in many ways belongs to the psychiatrist, and even with his or her help it still will remain a deep mystery.

Rejection is always connected with the rejection of Christ. One cannot get away from the firm hold that emotion has. It appears to grow bigger and bigger and fold a person in its arms. Many people have doubts, are filled with loneliness, and are subject to rejection. But rejection has a special meaning because it has been, as it were, the pilgrim who walked with Christ.

Christ's pilgrimage throughout Palestine was a real pilgrimage. He started, as many pilgrims do, with the desert, with the *poustinia*; then he went out from the desert to preach the gospel. But all around him, rejection stood as if transfigured. It walked with him, and it sat at his table. It was with him on the terrible day of the cross, from the palace to Golgotha. Rejection walked side by side with him to the cross.

Just stop for a moment and think. His hands were nailed to wood, and the hammer hit the soft flesh. As the hammer fastened both hands and feet, rejection arose in all its actuality and manifested itself, for here was God crucified and rejected by men. This is really something to ponder, a mystery before which one must prostrate oneself, and adore God. It is also something to cry about. Yet, at the same time, deep down in our heart, we know that his rejection is a healing for ours.

I am healed by his rejection. Very few people who are rejected think of Christ, but they should, for, from Gethsemani to the cross, and through all his life, rejection always whispered into his ear. It is not easy to understand the mystery of rejection, because it is so connected with Christ, so deeply engrained in him, almost a part of him. Still, it is obvious that if you or I place ourselves next to Christ and accept, or at least try to understand, the rejection which he underwent, we shall be healed.

A psychiatrist may help us, but what really will help us will be to enter into that immense mystery of Christ's rejection by everyone (except his mother and a few others). Incredible, is it not, that his pain is the healing oil of the Good Samaritan. We should meditate on this more often, because in his rejection is our physical and spiritual health.

Meditation 9

Rejection is often like a mirror. Perhaps it is part of our examination of conscience. But be that as it may, I go over my rejections at night and I discover that I have been rejected many times in a thousand little ways that don't really amount to much at the moment, but still hurt even as a little pinprick hurts. In the evening, however, I find that all the little pinpricks do turn into a larger wound and it really hurts. Examining our conscience is very important because we might be very angry at all those who have rejected us in so many small instances.

Take for instance just saying, "Good morning," or "Good afternoon," or "Good evening." How often we greet someone in the family with these usual greetings, and he or she fails to respond. This is a type of silence that can hurt us deeply, and yet we cannot say that it is a big thing.

Or let us consider a mother sitting and resting in the evening. She has worked hard all day for the good of the family, and she is tired. Around her are her teenage daughters. She is sitting there, thinking of how nice it would be to have a cup of tea with lemon. She is tired, her feet are swollen. The weight of the kitchen and the rest of the house—only three rooms—appears immense. She cannot tackle anything more. But not a single one of her daughters thinks that her mother, who usually has a cup of tea by herself, needs help to get the tea. The mother feels rejected. A pinprick, but how deep is that pinprick, how deep is that hurt!

Again, two girl friends are going to the movies. One is outgoing and dynamic, the other is shy and timid. The latter needs some help from the other who has all the qualities to attract other people, to be somebody. Desperately she hangs on to this friend of hers; suddenly, half way down to the theater, that brilliant friend says to her, "Look, don't bother me so much. Don't hang on me so much. You're a pest."

A few words dropped in the silence of timidity become more than pinpricks. They become a hot flame that sears. The rejection seems complete. The timid one says nothing, but as they approach the theater, she turns and runs away. The brilliant one looks after her, shaking her head; she doesn't realize what she has done. Little things . . . The evening comes on slowly; there is a heap of rejection to confront.

Here we considered only a few types of rejection. But let each one of my readers ponder if they have been rejected during the day, in a thousand little things.

The examination of conscience should proceed side by side with those rejections. Both the rejected and rejectee, those who are rejected and those who reject them, should make a profound examination of conscience. Rejecting anyone is a breach of charity, but not only of charity, also of faith. We directly deny, and brazenly, too, the words of Christ, "Whatever you do to the least of my brethren you do to me."

There are also his words to love one another. The rejected must look deep into their soul, and realize that they should not flee from harsh words, nor from pinpricks of rejection through the day. No, on the contrary, they should welcome them because through them they participate in Christ's rejection. There is one tremendous truth in all this: one of the ways that Christ saved us was by allowing himself to be rejected by man. Think of that seriously—God came from heaven to save us, and we rejected him!

Rise from the contemplation of your rejections, lift up your hands to heaven, and say to God, "Lord, I want to be rejected too, to share your rejection." And the moment that you have said this, I will hear your laughter, because the joy of God accepting your little sacrifice will transform itself into laughter.

Meditation 10

There are rejections, and there are rejections. In our age and time, some rejections are cataclysmic.

Take one for instance. I was rejected by my homeland—Russia—when revolution broke out. Only those who have experienced this kind of rejection can fully understand its immense power and its infinite tragedy. There was the revolution: it rejected the so-called aristocracy, the establishment, and hunted down the opposition. I read often today about South Africa, and other countries where people are killed by the thousands. I think of Russia. Ours was among the first of the great revolutions after the French Revolution; ten million refugees left Russia. How many were killed before and after Stalin would run into millions.

One leaves his country. He becomes a refugee—that is, if he is able to save himself. If not, he dies. He flees the fatherland, the one he loves, the one that means so much to him. He was born in it; he absorbed everything about its customs and ways. Suddenly he is compelled to enter a strange and foreign world. It is then that rejection uses its most powerful weapons.

I think I can comprehend something of what our Lady felt when her Son was killed. I had to witness the killing of many Russian sons, of my Russian brothers, many fathers and mothers. The sword that Simeon spoke of to Mary, penetrated all of Russia. We became strangers in a strange land. The country might have been wonderful to us, but it was no longer our own.

Our rejection was extreme. It shook us. It permeated our nights, and filled our dreams, as well as our conversations by day. Often, we gathered some place where Russian was spoken and recalled the days of old. At such moments one remembers something else too, or at least should remember. One remembers that Jesus was a refugee, and so was his mother and foster father. In faith, one plunges into the exile of Jesus from his land into the land of Egypt. Somehow, our exile from our land then becomes more understandable.

We refugees are making up what is wanting in the sufferings of Christ. St. Paul's words are a mystery in themselves, but refugees probe that mystery to its very depth.

Then, there are the Jews. They were rejected by everyone. A strange nation for centuries rejected by the ignorance of mankind. When you consider them there is something that comes from your heart that is very deep and profound. To be rejected by the majority of mankind must be terrible.

I recall my father talking about this; he often opened his doors to Jews who were victims of this rejection. He used to say to me and our family, "Always be kind to the Jews, because they are the rejected ones. Don't ever forget that out of their bosom came Jesus Christ, Mary, the mother of God and the Apostles."

But then you have to face Auschwitz, if you can. Words fail here. The Nazis not only rejected the Jews, but made martyrs out of them. The Jews believed in one God, Yahweh, and they were made martyrs for that belief. Their martyrdom earned them the land of their forefathers.

But then, consider the Arabs. Strange as it might seem, they in turn are being rejected by the Jewish people. A pain comes into your heart when two Semitic people are feuding with one another. There should be room for both in that ancient land. The mystery of this incomprehensible rejection begins to overwhelm you.

There are revolutions all over the world. The rejection of the Jews by the Nazis. The rejection of the Arabs by the Jews. And then, if you have strength to open your eyes and look across the world, what do you see?

In almost every nation, you see the rejection in one form or another. Much rejection today is motivated by anger. It becomes impossible to open your eyes, because there are few countries where this ultimate, cataclysmic rejection is not operative.

After witnessing such total rejection we have to stand at the side of Christ, take his hand and say, "Lord, have mercy on us. We really have sinned. We have substituted hatred for love; the love which You gave us as Your last commandment, has been turned into hate. Have mercy on us, Lord."

other writings by
Catherine de Hueck Doherty

Apostolic Farming
Dearly Beloved -- 3 volumes
Dear Father
Dear Seminarian
Fragments of My Life
Grace in Every Season
The Gospel of a Poor Woman
The Gospel Without Compromise
Journey Inward
Molchanie
Lubov
My Heart and I
My Russian Yesterdays
Not Without Parables
Our Lady's Unknown Mysteries
Poustinia
Re-entry into Faith
Sobornost
Soul of My Soul
Stations of the Cross
Strannik
Urodivoi
Welcome, Pilgrim

available through Madonna House Publications